VOICES
FROM
EL
SALVADOR

VOICES
FROM
EL
SALVADOR

From the original Spanish edition,

EL SALVADOR:
UNA AUTENTICA GUERRA CIVIL

MARIO MENENDEZ RODRIGUEZ

SOLIDARITY
PUBLICATIONS
P.O. Box 40874
San Francisco, California 94140 U.S.A.

Library of Congress Catalogue Card No. 81 - 86681
ISBN: 0-942638-04-2

First Printing April 1983
Second Printing June 1983
Printed in the U.S.A. by Popular Press

To order additional copies of this book, please write:
>SOLIDARITY PUBLICATIONS
>P.O. Box 40874
>San Francisco, California 94140

Please add 15% for postage and handling ($1.00 minimum).
Bulk discounts available. Write for a complete list of our
materials.

Editor: Adam Kufeld
Production Manager: Marlene Tobias
Distribution Manager: Holly Peck

Distributed in the United Kingdom by:
Third World Publications
151 Stratford Rd.
Birmingham B11 1RD
England

Editor's Note: On April 12, 1983 Salvador Cayetano Carpio, upon
learning that Mélida Anaya Montes, "Ana María," second-in command
of the Popular Forces of Liberation "Farabundo Martí" (FPL), had
been assassinated by another member of the Central Command along
with five other members of his organization, "suffered an emotional
crisis" and took his own life.

Leadership of the FPL has been passed on to Commander Salvador
Guerra. He has been directing the FPL forces in the province of
Chalatenango and serving on the FMLN General Staff for the Central
and Para-central Fronts.

VOICES
FROM
EL
SALVADOR

Thanks to:

Mario Menendez Rodriguez and Editorial Universitaria Centroamericana, EDUCA, for their permission to reprint this book.

We would also like to thank Beth Henson and Bonnie Weissman for the typesetting; Dennis Jennings and John Benson for the camera work; Paula Kristovich for the layout, and all the photographers who generously donated photographs and to all those who lent valuable financial assistance.

SOLIDARITY PUBLICATIONS is a not-for-profit organization that has been publishing materials from the revolutionary movements in El Salvador and Central America since 1980. Our aim is to make widely available the thoughts and writings of the Central American people as they struggle to create new and democratic societies.

We welcome contributions of any size to help with this effort. If you wish to make a tax-deductable donation please contact us at: Solidarity Publications, P.O. Box 40874, S.F., CA. 94140

CONTENTS

This book is dedicated to all those who have given their lives
in the quest for a new El Salvador.

INTRODUCTION / AN UPDATE

Until recently few people had heard of El Salvador. Today the Salvadoran revolution commands the attention of the entire world.

The commitment of the Salvadoran people to struggle for a better life has inspired millions. But their determination has sparked a violent response from those who would attempt to hold back the advance of humanity. To defend a system which profits from the impoverishment of others, the United States Government has committed itself to an alliance with one of the most barbaric "governments" history has known. The tortures and massacres often go far beyond the worst that one can imagine. We can say without exaggeration that a genocidal war is being waged against the people of El Salvador with the full support of the U.S. government, all in the name of anti-communism. But history does not forget crimes of this magnitude, nor does it forget the criminals.

When the interviews contained here were first published, the Salvadoran people were taking the first concrete steps to unite their forces. These steps led to the founding of the Farabundo Martí Front for National Liberation, the FMLN, which today fights for the liberation of El Salvador.

The key event leading to the formation of the FMLN was the December 17, 1979 founding of the Political Military Coordinator, bringing together three of today's five political-military organizations: the Popular Forces of Liberation "Farabundo Martí" (FPL), National Resistance (RN) and the Communist Party of El Salvador (PCS). This was followed by the uniting of the four revolutionary mass organizations—the Popular Revolutionary Bloc (BPR), the Popular United Action Front (FAPU), the February 28th Popular Leagues (LP-28) and the Democratic Nationalist Union (UDN)—to form the Revolutionary Coordinator of the Masses (CRM) in January of 1980. On April 18th the CRM joined other democratic organizations to form the Democratic Revolutionary Front (FDR), the broadest coalition ever in the long history of popular struggle in El Salvador. On October 10th the three previously mentioned political-military organizations and the People's Revolutionary Army (ERP) united their forces and formed the FMLN. And in the beginning of 1981 the Revolutionary Party of Central American Workers (PRTC) also joined the FMLN.

The year 1980 also witnessed mass demonstrations of unity and strength. On January 22, 300,000 people took to the streets to celebrate the founding of the CRM and the anniversary of the 1932 insurrection. On June 24th and 25th a successful general strike took place throughout the country. All these manifestations of the people's strength were brutally attacked, resulting in hundreds of deaths. Even the funeral march of the assassinated Archbishop Oscar Romero was fired on by government troops.

These were to be the last open demonstrations in El Salvador. The November 27, 1980 kidnapping, torture and assassination of six leaders of the FDR was one more clear statement of the junta's strategy: an all-out war against the people of El Salvador, which has taken the lives of more than 43,000 people since 1979.

On January 10, 1981 the political-military organizations of El Salvador, united in the FMLN, launched a general offensive throughout the country.

Since then the strength of the FMLN/FDR has increased, and despite the U.S. government's massive military aid to the junta, the FMLN forces have not been defeated in any of the major offensives against them. Moreover, with their political-military advances they have struck serious blows at the oligarchy and military structure, and become the major challenge to U.S. policy in Central America.

Additionally, the establishment by the FMLN of zones of control in over 20 percent of the national territory is the concrete expression of the people's determination to create the new El Salvador. In these zones, young and old learn to read and write, health needs are met for the first time, women become equal partners in struggle and an alternative economy takes shape.

With the strategy of "resist, develop and advance," the FMLN demonstrates the heroism, courage and persistance of a people determined to win.

Voices from El Salvador traces the development of El Salvador's political-military organizations through the clear and decisive words of their most beloved leaders. This book provides a vision of the humanity of the Salvadoran people, offering hope and inspiration for all progressive and revolutionary people dedicated to the building of a new world.

—*Adam Kufeld*
SOLIDARITY PUBLICATIONS

I
A People
At War

A People At War

A real civil war, becoming less and less irregular and intermittent and more and more relentless, is tearing apart the smallest country in Central America, the scene of a drama of extraordinary, unforeseeable dimensions.

The polarization of the class struggle has reached an acute stage, and economic, political, legal, ideological, cultural and spiritual relations are in deep, irreversible crisis.

Social contradictions are at a point of maximum tension.

Military combats of a certain scope are taking place in cities and towns, the development of the People's Liberation Army is an indisputable fact, and the actions of the guerrilla movement cover the entire national territory. On a smaller scale, in villages and hamlets, militia groups are striving to guarantee the establishment of a new, revolutionary power, which has the support and trust of the majority of the population.

The next few months are expected to witness the crystallization of popular insurrections in different localities, insurrections which, through the very dynamics of events, will generate general insurrection, the insurrection of an entire people who have said "Enough!" to oppression.

PRENSA LATINA: SINGULAR WITNESS TO HISTORY

Since the end of December, 1979, during a journey of several weeks through this nation whose foundations are cracked by uncontainable violence, the writer has been forced to engage in a round-the-clock duel with death.

For this series of articles to be written where history is in the making, it has been necessary to slip through the encirclements of the military dictatorship, in the midst of heavy firing; steer clear of the sudden checks and searches on any street in San Salvador, on the highways and in cities and towns throughout the country; get used to communication through sign language and precise contacts; to long hours of silence; and to staying calm a meter away from killers looking uneasy, their fingers on the triggers of G-3's.

If the writer had been caught with one of his notebooks on the situation in El Salvador, or, with a roll of film containing photographs of the important sixth meeting of the Revolutionary Council of the Farabundo Martí Popular Liberation Forces, it would have meant certain death.

However, thanks to the efficacy of the revolutionary and democratic movement in El Salvador, to the unquestionable and determined support of an heroic people, a total of 90 hours of interviews and unprecedented military actions were taped and some 1600 pictures taken.

14 FAMILIES FORCE VIOLENCE ON PEOPLE

Peaceful ways of solving the serious difficulties facing five million people have been definitively closed off by the Hill, Dueñas, Regalado, Wright, Guirola, Sol, Daglio, De Sola, Quiñónes, Llack, Borja, García Pireto, Salaverria and Meza Ayau families, that is, by those who control the Salvadoran economy: finances, banking, industry, credit, the big export-import business and the domestic buying of coffee, cotton and sugar from small and middle growers.

Unquestionably, as the Catholic Church headed by Archbishop Oscar Arnulfo Romero has reiterated on more than one day, violence has been forced upon the Salvadoran people, by the notorious fourteen families of feudal mentality, insatiable and insolent, ignorant, unbending and criminal, whose armed forces, special security bodies and numerous paramilitary bands shed blood over a geographical area of just 20,000 square kilometers.

In the streets of El Salvador, in broad daylight, the reporter witnessed veritable witchhunts for human beings. He saw hundreds of children and old people, men and women of all ages, under "institutional" gunfire for the "crime" of demanding bread, jobs, housing, education, health, the right to freedom and democracy.

In villages, cantons, estates and factories, I saw the hideously mutilated bodies of peasants and workers; more than a few of them had their chopped-off genitals stuck in their mouths, their eyes and tongues torn out and their faces and fingers burned by muriatic acid. Others had been beheaded and the heads placed on view for the local population.

The climate of terror is indescribable.

World public opinion may find it hard to imagine that in a country where 95 percent of the population profess the Catholic religion, priests are tortured and murdered for promoting the full liberation of man; that the faces of catechism students and those enrolled in Christianity courses, people whose cause and reason for being is devotion to others, are flayed by sharp knives; or that worshippers are gunned down inside their churches.

None of this is an exaggeration.

In the martyred, heroic land of the Aguilares - three brothers, priests who played an outstanding role in early 19th century independence struggles against Spanish colonial rule - the bullets of automatic rifles hidden in the bush destroyed the body of a venerable Jesuit, Rutilio Grande, when he was on his way home after visiting a household in mourning due to rightwing terror. He was sacrificed to Moloch, "in the name of National Security."

In San Vicente, parish priest Alirio Macías was riddled with bullets by members of one of the fascist bands serving the fourteen families: ORDEN (Nationalist Democratic Organization).

In the bloody streets of San Salvador, priest Octavio Ortiz made the sign of the cross and begged for mercy for people wounded in a demonstration. The killers did not heed his pleas, they were not moved by the tears of the man of God: a light tank crushed him to death. The bodies of other victims were also flattened by armored vehicles.

The name of Rafael Palacios has been added to the list of priests murdered by the fascists, as has that of Alfonso Navarro Oviedo, executed in the Miramonte Monastery. The fourteen families accused this noted leader of Christianity courses of having helped organize rural and city wage earners.

The case of Ernesto Barrera Moto shook the pillars of Salvadoran social conscience with even greater force, because this exemplary priest chose armed struggle, joined the Farabundo Martí Popular Liberation Forces and died in unequal combat against the regime's repressive bodies.

Mexican nun María Esther López' life was saved because the killers felt that as a foreigner it was politically wiser to merely deport her.

However, among the savage crimes that have shaken public opinion and the Catholic Church in general, Archbishop Romero in particular, special stress is placed on the killings of Apolinario Serrano (Polín), founder and general secretary of the Christian Federation of Salvadoran Peasants (FECCAS), bastion of the Popular Revolutionary Bloc (BPR), the principal mass organization in El Salvador, and Felipe de Jesús Chacón, outstanding leader of the Christianity Courses Movement and father of BPR general secretary, Juan Chacón Vásquez.

The killers' hatred and fear of these persons, "essentially good and very much loved by the people," to quote the Archbishop of San Salvador during an exclusive interview with Prensa Latina, were reflected in their unrecognizable bodies. Suffice it to say that

Felipe de Jesús was not only shot; his face heralding the new human being was flayed; his eyes that had witnessed countless crimes and the tongue with which he had denounced the fourteen families were cut out.

The Salvadorean people were left with no course but that of revolutionary violence in reply to ultrarightwing terror. And they have opted, after having exhausted all peaceful means, for wielding the legitimate, supreme right of insurrection.

ECONOMIC AND SOCIAL SYNTHESIS

Today more than ever before the dispossessed are determined to destroy the old, outworn economic, political and social structures of the prison-country which for close to half a century has been under the yoke of an implacable military dictatorship, guardian of the interests of the oligarchy and foreign capital, and where:

Less than half of one percent of the owners possess 37.3 percent of the arable land while 91.4 percent own 21.9 percent.

Fifty-eight percent of the population have less than ten dollars a month to "live on."

Sixty percent of the Salvadoreans living in rural areas and 40 percent of those living in the cities cannot read or write.

■ Just 16 percent of the economically active population work all year round.

There are less than three doctors per 10,000 inhabitants and most of the country's 1300 doctors are concentrated in the capital.

There are under two hospital beds per thousand inhabitants while there are no reliable infant mortality data.

Population density is 200 per square kilometer, and in San Salvador over 200,000 people exist in subhuman conditions - with cardboard or newspaper covering, no plumbing facilities, running water or electricity.

In such a setting, even minor struggles to back wage demands become grave social conflicts.

UNITY OF THE REVOLUTIONARY AND DEMOCRATIC FORCES

The relentless advance of the Salvadorean people takes on greater thrust because for the first time the most outstanding revolutionary political-military organizations - the Farabundo Martí Popular Liberation Forces, the Communist Party of El Salvador, the Armed Forces of National Resistance and the People's Revolutionary Army (ERP) are acting together.

At the same time this unity of action also extends, in actual practice, to the main mass organizations: the Popular Revolutionary Bloc (BPR), the 28th of February People's Leagues, the Unitary Popular Action Front (FAPU) and the Democratic Nationalist Union (UDN), organizations with which important Catholic Church and social democratic sectors cooperate, as well as the realistic, progressive sector of the Christian Democratic Party and an unknown number of young military men who for security reasons act with great caution.

The horizon of unity among revolutionary and democratic forces broadens with the process of social liberation, which also includes the Revolutionary Party of Salvadoran Workers and the People's Liberation Movement, both founded in 1979, and other leagues and groups.

In demonstrations, in the armed occupation of cities, towns, cantons, estates and factories, the indispensable coordination leading to the qualitative development of the revolutionary process is evident.

FOREIGN INTERVENTION

Zbigniew Brzezinski, national security advisor of United States President James Carter, does not hide his concern over the revolutionary situation in El Salvador, especially after the failure of the first government junta, which lasted slightly over two months, and the lack of popular support for the "new" attempt to deal with the crisis. The "new" attempt is that of the armed forces, "represented" by Colonels José Guillermo García, Jaime Abdul Gutiérrez (both with close ties to the CIA), and Adolfo Arnoldo Majano, in alliance with the right-wing sector of the Christian Democratic Party headed by engineer José Napoleón Duarte.

The appointment of Robert White, advisor for several years to Paraguayan dictator Alfredo Stroessner and specialist in counterinsurgency, as ambassador; the visit by Assistant Secretary of State for Inter-American Affairs William Bowdler; and the arrival of more than a few Pentagon officials coincide with the incorporation of several thousand U.S., Saigonese, Guatemalan and counterrevolutionary Cuban mercenaries into the ranks of private armies at the service of the fourteen families and with stepped-up repression in El Salvador.

The repressive high command, clandestine in nature, includes Washington advisors; generals such as Jose Alberto Medrano, colonels such as José Guillermo García; majors such as Roberto D' Aubuisson; and the financial groups of the Cuscatlan Bank and the Popular Credit Bank, both associated with foreign capital - especially U.S. capital. The command coordinates not only the operations of private armies but also the activities of the National Security Agency (ANSESAL), the National Guard, the customs, treasury and national police, the army's Counterinsurgency School - located in San Francisco Gotera in Morazan department in the eastern part of the country - the Engineering School of the Armed Forces (CIIFA) - located in Zacatecoluca, La Paz department in the central region - and ORDEN - which in turn maintains ties with the Guatemalan "National Liberation Movement" headed by mass murderer Mario Sandoval Alarcón.

The linkup of an infinitesimal part of the fortunes of the fourteen families -especially the Hill, Regalado and Dueñas families - with the "National Security" experience of the fascist military is hidden behind corporations set up for that purpose with the support of the Cuscatlan Bank and the Popular Credit Bank into which the Central Bank funnels over half of the financial resources of the Salvadoran state.

Week after week large shipments of arms for the private armies and special bodies of the ultraright, plus the "institutional" forces, arrive from Miami and Guatemala. And Ilopango International Airport shifts its civil operations to Comalapa in order to become exclusively a strategic military air force center. In the past few days it has received from the United States combat helicopters for counterinsurgency combat.

Meanwhile the United States Government, in agreement with that of Honduras, where the Francisco Morazán National Liberation Front is active, has mined the main highways along the Honduran border with El Salvador and Nicaragua.

THE STRATEGIC DOMINO

Unquestionably, El Salvador is the United States' strategic domino in the Central American game. If it falls, according to Pentagon thinking, Guatemala and Honduras would not be far behind.

But if the Salvadoran revolutionary movement is defeated in the decisive clashes of the next few months, then the armed forces of international neofascism would intervene in Nicaragua.

Within the cold war setting of recent weeks, the dynamics of events in El Salvador could mean an important change in U.S. policy regarding Latin America. Hence, a direct armed intervention against the homeland of Agustín Farabundo Martí (labor leader killed during the 1932 slaughter) first with the participation of the regular armies of Guatemala and Honduras and then, or perhaps at the same time, of special U.S. operative divisions stationed in the Caribbean.

The Pentagon has its cards on the table, as demonstrated by General Robert Schweitzer, one of its specialists in armed interventions.

INTERNATIONAL SOLIDARITY

In 1932 El Salvador was the scene of a popular insurrection that was crushed by the regime of General Maximiliano Hernández Martínez. The toll of blood for the attempt to storm the heavens of freedom, democracy, independence and social justice was extraordinary: over 30,000 dead, among peasants, workers, students and other sectors.

Since then Latin America in particular and progressive governments and peoples of the world in general have a debt of solidarity with the heroic Salvadoran people whose impressive, just struggle of today, after close to half a century, is entering a decisive, difficult stage.

People of good faith have the floor.

An FPL women's meeting in Chalatenango province.

II
With the
"Farabundo Marti"
Popular Liberation
Forces (F.P.L.)

SALVADOR CAYETANO CARPIO
"MARCIAL"

Salvador Cayetano Carpio: Commander-in-Chief

Salvador Cayetano Carpio, a name that means a great deal in Central America, is neither dead nor living abroad: he is the top leader of the Farabundo Martí Popular Liberation Forces.

He is also Comrade "Marcial" in the underground.

For ten years the identity of the top leader of the most important revolutionary political-military organization in this small nation at war was unknown. Likewise, the fate of the most prestigious working class leader, whose life sums up the past 40 years of struggle of the Salvadorean people, was unknown. He had left behind the dividing line between reality and the people's imagination, and had become a legend.

The name of Salvador Cayetano Carpio is not spoken out loud; for the dispossessed, it is a very intimate thing, something that is all their own, a hope for redemption; for the fourteen families and the guardians of their wealth, it means conscience and a warning of the inevitable end of social injustice.

As Prensa Latina reveals the truth about the exceptional revolutionary in an exclusive interview that took several days, the key questions about the economic, social, political and military situation in El Salvador begin to be answered.

It can be said with certainty that the disclosures about Salvador Cayetano Carpio will speed up the process of the definitive liberation of the Salvadoreans, not only because they will inspire greater confidence in the dispossessed masses but also will help to strengthen further the unity of the revolutionary and democratic forces. In addition, they will mean a telling psychological blow to the oligarchy and the leaders of the ultraright-wing terrorist bands, including General José Alberto Medrano who personally directed savage tortures on more than a few occasions, on the man who is now revealed as the commander in chief of the Popular Liberation Armed Forces.

Virtually everyone in El Salvador is familiar with the dedication and leadership qualities of Salvador Cayetano Carpio, whose sacrifices for the happiness of his people know no limits, beginning with his suffering over the murder of his family, with whose blood pages of the history of this country have been written.

In the House of the Teachers in San Salvador, this writer saw a "revolutionary altar" to Emma Guadalupe Carpio Rosales, killed in the streets of the capital on May 22, 1979. The 15th Congress of the June 21 National Association of Teachers bore the name of this mother of three girls who in 1946 was "adopted, supported and educated by the working class" because her father, Salvador Cayetano Carpio, then leader of the bakers union, was in prison and after that relentlessly persecuted.

A BIT OF BACKGROUND

The 60-year-old revolutionary, with the strong physique characteristic of the workers of Indian America, displays great modesty that probably stems from his life alongside his grandparents in an old peoples' home; his path towards the priesthood (when he studied in the Conciliar Seminary) which was later interrupted; and in his first strikes and struggles as a labor leader for the most indispensable things: food, shelter, clothing, etc.

It must be said that those same revolutionary virtues of "Marcial" also typify the members of the Farabundo Martí FPL who include, in addition to workers, peasants, teachers and students, former priests, seminarists, catechists and people enrolled in Christianity courses. When the latter are asked for their reasons for joining the organization, they inevitably reply that, in addition to political reasons, it's because of the human relations, the serious approach to work, and the generosity of the members....

THREE DAYS WITH THE "HO CHI MINH OF LATIN AMERICA"

Strict security measures colored the setting of the meetings with Salvador Cayetano Carpio, held in different places in the country.

Outstanding among the surprises awaiting the writer in the course of the interview with Salvador Cayetano Carpio, over a three-day period, was the extent the political-military organization has taken root among the people, and it was this factor that guaranteed personal security and the success of the effort....

Children, women, old people stood guard, and not only ten or 100 meters away but several kilometers from the places where we met.

Thus the members of the first group of "peripheral security" were to announce the presence of the repressive forces by setting off a bomb and then the emergency measures would immediately have gone into effect to guarantee our withdrawal.

But there was no need to do so, because the zones we were in are organized politically, by the party of the organization, and militarily, by the army, the guerrillas and the militia, that is, by the Popular Liberation Armed Forces.

In addition, the mass organizations in those places are supervised by the Popular Revolutionary Bloc (BPR).

EXILED IN MEXICO: WORKING IN MERIDA

"For a short time," Salvador Cayetano Carpio remarked before we began to record the interview, "I was in Mexico. I worked in the place you're from, in Yucatán. Mérida is very pretty and the people there are hospitable....but I had to return to my country to continue the struggle...."

The security chief of the FPL had said we had four hours for the first interview and he warned that the security measures should be followed to the letter.

The message seemed aimed at the journalist since "Marcial" is one of those leaders who have great respect for discipline and are the first to set an example, never demanding more of others than they do of themselves.

And so we began the interview to answer ten years' worth of questions....

THE FARABUNDO MARTI FPL IN APRIL, 1970

When and why was the Farabundo Martí FPL founded?

"The beginning of the work to organize it goes back to April 1, 1970, which means that this year it will be a decade ago. It came into being as a necessity of the revolutionary process of our people, a process that, having reached a certain level in the class struggle, required forging political and organizational instruments capable of implementing their struggle in an integral way in all spheres....This historical necessity arose after a long process of ideological struggle within the traditional organizations when it became evident that they stubbornly refused to lead the working class and the people in general in the new stages of struggle that needed to be undertaken....Concretely, the traditional organizations denied the possibility and necessity of the Salvadorean people undertaking the process of revolutionary armed struggle. They also denied the mounting element of revolutionary violence in the struggles of the broad popular masses....

"Now then, within the Communist Party of El Salvador and the organizations influenced by it, if there hadn't arisen a stubborn majority that at all costs blocked the advance towards the political-military strategy that the people needed for moving towards new stages of struggle, no need would have arisen to create a revolutionary organization such as the Farabundo Martí Popular Liberation Forces, which rapidly incorporated broad sectors of the people into all forms of struggle.

"Life has shown that the advance of the process of class struggle cannot be stopped with dogmatic formulas, which, at a given point, no longer correspond to objective reality and the historical need for social development. That is the reason the Farabundo Martí Popular Liberation Forces came into being.

"Before it was founded, I repeat, it was necessary to wage within the Communist Party and other organizations an ideological struggle that took many years: it began virtually with the victory of the Cuban Revolution, when the most clear-sighted people in those organizations began to feel that a dogmatic line could not lead the revolutionary process into the new stages that were required....

"By the end of 1969 it was very clear that El Salvador, its people, needed an overall strategy in which all methods of struggle could be used and combined in dialectical fashion, and that armed struggle would be the main thread running through the people's revolutionary fervor and would become in the process the basic element for the destruction of the counterrevolutionary forces....

"So, in reaching that conviction, the most clear-sighted people, who at that moment understood the needs of the revolutionary struggle in our country, had to withdraw from the organizations to which they had virtually devoted their lives, with a great deal of pain but with great realism in taking the step....Thus it was necessary to create more effective instruments of struggle for the people....To do so it was necessary to leave posts of great responsibility and honor in those other organizations.

"Several of our members who later joined the Farabundo Martí Popular Liberation Forces as founding members were esteemed leaders of the workers movement. For instance, José Dimas Alas was the secretary general of the Labor Unity Federation and one of its founders; Comrade Ernesto Morales was the youth secretary of the same Federation; and there were others who were also labor leaders who had to leave the traditional organizations to be able to develop in the new revolutionary school....In my own case I resigned as general secretary of the Communist Party of El Salvador, a post I had held for a number of years. I made the move when it became evident that it wasn't possible to get the Party to understand the need for a political-military strategy, that is, an overall revolutionary strategy, and that this had to be demonstrated to our people in practice....Once the correctness of the political-military strategy was demonstrated in practice, when it was clear it could no longer be denied, the different honest forces in the country could find in the new organization a point of contact on a new basis....

"In other words, after it was demonstrated that revolutionary struggle was - and is - the only course, then and only then was it possible to seek other paths in the direction of greater unity....

"And it is through the efforts of the Farabundo Martí Popular Liberation Forces, through the efforts of many comrades killed in struggle over the past ten years, that it has been clearly demonstrated that the political-military revolutionary strategy of prolonged war has enabled our people to advance to a stage in which no honest person in El Salvador can fail to recognize that it is the only course for the definitive liberation of our people."

WE HAD TO FIND OUT IF WE COULD MAKE THE GRADE

However, in the first two years, that is 1970 to 1972, the organization today known as the Farabundo Martí FPL went without a name. Why was that?

"That was an easy decision to make, and we made it at the first meeting of our organization for reasons that we regarded then as basic for becoming revolutionaries with a new discipline, forged in the sacrifices required by the course we were adopting, that of prolonged war, a course that had not been tried in our country....

"We needed to find out if we were capable of promoting that course and if we ourselves as people were going to succeed in following that course, if we would be able to acquire enough strength and make the necessary sacrifices, give up normal life for an underground existence and cope with strict compartmentalization....

"That is, we needed to be tempered in the crucible of practice. You can say it was a test to see if we were capable of putting theory into practice. And only practical experience could give us the answer....

"Moreover, in previous years, in El Salvador there had been a lot of theory, and we had fought against the theories of the armchair revolutionaries....So we had to prove that we weren't going to be revolutionaries in word alone. The course was difficult and unknown; we had to find out if we could make the grade.

"In the second place, we were deeply influenced by the appearance in the 60's of a number of organizations with the good intentions of taking the road of the guerrilla struggle in the mountains; they would immediately speak of those aspirations to internationalist comrades from other countries, who helped them fraternally, so they could carry out the revolutionary project in El Salvador....However, after a short time, it became clear that those groups broke up, that they splintered....

"We needed to leave that formula behind, and so, for the first while, we didn't ask for aid of any kind from our comrades abroad. That's because we didn't feel that we had in practice lived the revolutionary life that would mean we were deserving of being recognized as revolutionaries....There was a third factor involved; we needed not only to prove ourselves and forge the initial group and the cells that began to form around our organization, we also needed our people to begin to recognize through actual practice that a serious revolutionary organization had emerged, one that was prepared to conduct the revolutionary struggle in all respects....That was why we decided not to adopt a name until our people recognized the organization because of its political and military importance....

"That was decided between August and September, 1972, when some of our dearest founding comrades had already shed their blood fighting the enemy. Their deaths shook the people, who saw how exemplary those comrades were in their readiness to give their lives for the people's cause. That spirit of determination, of devotion was recognized by the Salvadorean people....

"Moreover, we had already conducted some actions in solidarity, international solidarity. For instance after the Trelew murders, we blew up the Argentine embassy. Another series of actions against imperialism were carried out and our people were shaken by the possibility and the existence of an organization that was emerging as using all methods of struggle.

"Then, once that point had been reached, we had to inform the people of our existence: the Farabundo Martí Popular Liberation Forces also began to influence and conduct propaganda among the masses....Our objective was to build a broad mass movement...."

THE PEOPLE SHOULD KNOW SOME OF THEIR LEADERS

After ten years this is the first disclosure of the identity of the top leader of the central command of the Farabundo Martí Popular Liberation Forces. What are the reasons for this?

"This is a natural thing in our organization. Due to its characteristic of being an underground, compartmentalized organization, no one is known by their real name. Even within the central command, the comrades who work daily in the top war command don't know each other's real names. Therefore, within the organization, the great majority of the comrades don't know my real identity....

"It is a rule of our organization that only in the context of the needs of our work are we to see each other's faces. And that has to be the case not only in regard to myself but also in regard to the cadres who direct the revolution in our organization....

"But there is another consideration: the members of our organization fuse with the organization into a single collective. Our work is collective and individual contributions become part of the patrimony of our organization. There is no need in that regard for people to be identified by their real name: what our organization requires are pseudonyms.

"So, because of the collective work, the compartmentalization, the rules of an underground existence and also for security reasons, it was very natural for my name not to be known....

"Now, for political reasons, the organization feels my name should be revealed. Those reasons have to do with the moment in which we are living and the need for the people to know some of their leaders."

The part of the past recounted by Salvador Cayetano Carpio is projected towards a qualitatively different present and demonstrates once again the dialectics of development through contradictions. For in a decisive moment for the process of social liberation, the Communist Party of El Salvador, today led by Schafik Jorge Handal, has earned the historical merit of offering an example of unity of action of the revolutionary and democratic forces that provided a great thrust to the revolution and deserved the recognition of the Salvadorean people.

The war approaches its final stages

"This war, which has now lasted ten years, is entering its final stages....We don't think it will be too long before a people's revolutionary government is set up, and if the United States steps in directly, El Salvador will be the grave of Yankee Marines," warned Salvador Cayetano Carpio, top leader of the Farabundo Martí Popular Liberation Forces.

In an exclusive interview for Excelsior*, "Comrade Marcial," champion of the political-military makeup of the Salvadorean revolution, unfolding in a strategy of prolonged popular war combining all forms and means of struggle, stressed that the time needed to attain the social liberation of this small nation depends essentially in developing and strengthening the unity of action of revolutionary and democratic forces.

AGUSTIN FARABUNDO MARTI AND NICARAGUA IN 1979

The organization bears the name of one who is a "lofty symbol in the history of El Salvador, Central America and Latin America."

Because Augustín Farabundo Martí, as Carpio pointed out, "has been the most outstanding revolutionary in the whole of our people's history. An exemplary inter-

---

* Editor's Note: Excelsior is the largest selling newspaper in Mexico.

nationalist, he fought alongside Sandino and his guerrillas in the Segovias in Nicaragua. Founder of the Communist Party in March 1930, two years later he headed a vast popular insurrection - which failed, due, among other reasons, to the following: limited development of the working class, ignorance of military arts, almost total lack of arms, military structures and leaders, a Party to which there was still no shape, which was taking its first steps, and with a basic weakness in its social composition...."

Agustín Farabundo Martí, taken prisoner due to an act of betrayal, was shot by General Maximiliano Hernandez Martinez in 1932, when over 30,000 Salvadoreans lost their lives.

However, the weaknesses and errors mentioned, which led to others that also played a role in the defeat of the popular movement, "were studied and analyzed carefully by our organization," explained Carpio, "and the teachings obtained from that heroic experience guide current revolutionary practice."

Suddenly Carpio fell silent....through his mind pass the names of the numerous martyrs who made the Farabundo Martí Popular Liberation Forces possible....He recalled the initial nucleus, the founders of the Salvadorean dawn....

And he added:

"The internationalist example of Agustín Farabundo Martí was reflected in actual practice during the struggle of the Sandinista people of Nicaragua against the savage Somoza dictatorship, when a brigade from our organization, under the name and red banner of the exemplary revolutionary, fought and shed their blood for the liberation of our beloved Nicaraguan brothers and sisters. Artillery men Luis, Neto, Morris and Quique were killed in action in Nicaragua in 1979 and posthumously named honorary councilors of the Farabundo Martí Popular Liberation Forces at our sixth meeting of the Revolutionary Council...."

In the early days, "when we had to prove ourselves in the revolutionary school and earn political and military recognition from the people," Carpio himself led and participated in armed actions. "And not only in the beginning, but afterwards, too, whenever there was need of certain operations."

POLITICAL ASYLUM "IS NOT A POLITICAL EXPEDIENT"

Due to the specific conditions of El Salvador (a small land area, crisscrossed by roads and with no high mountains, and with 200 inhabitants per square kilometer), one of the characteristics of the members of the Popular Liberation Forces is not to use political asylum.

"The struggle in our country is very hard, the repression constant," explained Carpio. "All revolutionaries are under threat day and night. Going out on the street is in itself a risk, a military operation almost....In addition, comrades must carry out their work and cover all sectors: among the masses, in the guerrilla, in the army, all over.... And so their lives are constantly in danger.

"Because of this, and precisely because of this, we have had to build up a sense of awareness, a mystique....Thus, the members of our organization are prepared to give their lives for the interests of the people at any time and under any circumstance, wherever necessary: at home in the city, when attacked by the repressive forces, in the country, night after night, when the special bodies and paramilitary bands of ORDEN attack and set fire to villages and hovels....For months on end, the comrades are forced to remain in hiding, far from their families...."

This writer has interviewed peasants, such as the Bellozos, the Rodriguezes and the Ramirezes, to mention just a few examples, who for eight years have not gone near a village, because the ultraright-wing hordes have threatened them with murder. People around must obtain for them all they need to survive.

Such a situation "inculcates a mystique, a sense of realizing that the struggle, in its very advanced stage, is going on here in the country, on every single millimeter of our soil. As a consequence, a psychosis of asylum has arisen, the idea being to leave El Salvador and thus escape death. And so, several thousand Salvadoreans, that is, the people who comprise the advanced sectors of our people, felt obliged to leave the country...."

The commander in chief of the Popular Liberation Armed Forces - army, guerrilla and militia - stressed:

"Revolutionaries must set an example and remain alongside their people, who are suffering the consequences of violent repression....Revolutionaries need to take advantage of difficult conditions in order to achieve a greater mastery over the methods and forms of clandestine struggle; they must become skilled in the art of conspiracy in order to better serve the Salvadorean oppressed masses.

"Because of that our organization holds that asylum is not a very positive expedient for the revolutionaries in El Salvador....There have been some exceptions, due to special situations, but they serve to confirm the rule...."

UNITY: A HISTORIC MILESTONE

In recent weeks, in the nation that is a key piece for United States' interests in Central America, a process of unity of action has been rapidly unfolding among the political-military revolutionary organizations and also among the mass organizations.

What is Carpio's opinion on unity and the prospects for it?

"The present steps of coordination in a gradual process of unity unquestionably represent a victory in the practice of our people's revolutionary struggle. A whole new stage is beginning in which the revolutionary and democratic forces will achieve, in a progressive, but progressively rapid and intensive fashion, in decisive phases, toward mutual revolutionary confidence and unity in various aspects.

"The recent agreement forged among the Farabundo Martí Popular Liberation Forces, the National Resistance and the Communist Party of El Salvador, an agreement consisting in the formation of a coordinating body for the start of a whole process of unity, is really a historic step, a far-reaching development for our people, an agreement that comes about precisely on the threshhold of increasingly intensive battles that are of mounting importance in terms of taking power.

"It can be said that the agreement is a historic milestone; it marks the status of the joint efforts of our entire people in order to finally crush oppression, poverty, hunger, the lack of democratic freedoms, repression, and to build a people's revolutionary government that will lay the groundwork for a just, human, fraternal society, one that will enable our country to be independent, one in which all sectors of our people will enjoy broad democratic freedoms....

"This process has cost the people a great deal of blood. Reaching an agreement on unity has meant in practice, over the years, testing the correctness of a strategy, one that has shown that dogmas, incorrect interpretations of our reality, had to be left behind and that all honest people in our country, all progressive people, finally had to reach the conclusion that in El Salvador the only course is popular revolution.

"On this basis, we have set out fully aware of what we are doing, with firm steps, on the road to the monolithic unity of all the people.

"It is the triumph of a strategy to put into practice by the people, a strategy in which hundreds and hundreds of the best patriots of our people have shed their blood for the interests of the exploited classes; a strategy in which the ruling classes have demonstrated all their cruelty and their incapacity when it comes to solving even the slightest problems confronting the masses of the people.

"In reaching the conviction that there is no more room for demagogic solutions, for phony variations on the theme that the imperialists are trying to implement, in alliance with their savage partners on the local scene, that is, the ruling classes and the hired guardians of their wealth; now that all this is clear, when no one can claim any more that there is any solution other than armed struggle, combined with all the other forms of people's struggle, there has been a rise in the level of awareness of all the organizations that want the happiness and well-being of our people, and it is on that higher basis that coordination has been put forward as the start to the process of revolutionary unity....

"Naturally, since the Salvadorean revolutionary organizations have had different origins and taken different courses in which they have been developing in parallel fashion, it can hardly be said that the road to higher unity is an easy process. Higher stages of unity would be organic unity in all spheres.

"However, there is one thing of which we can be sure: we who have realized that people's revolution is the only solution also realize that we must forge close unity to transform the popular movement into an uncontainable torrent that will sweep away oppression and exploitation.

"The revolutionary organizations and we who lead them are absolutely determined to consolidate, bolster and develop that unity, to raise it to increasingly higher stages, notwithstanding the difficulties that may present themselves in the process. If we have demonstrated that our people are capable of confronting all the offensives of imperialism and the ruling classes so far, we will also be capable of demonstrating that we are sufficiently mature as to succeed in solving any problem that may turn up on the road to the unity of the revolutionary and popular forces.

"So, even though the present moment involves initial steps in coordination, it must be clearly stated that they are based on a firm determination to advance in the most correct way possible, as intensely as possible, until all the hands of our people become a single hard-hitting fist....

"We believe that the time is not so far off when we will build a people's revolutionary government....Together, the people are marching forward, and there is no force capable of defeating them. No one and nothing will stop the liberation process of the Salvadorean people....

"Thus, these steps toward unity are firm, conscientious ones. In addition, we are determined to carry the process to its last consequences. Those steps represent the opening of a new chapter in the history of El Salvador and will determine the victory of the popular revolution and the advance towards socialism."

BROADER PEOPLE'S UNITY NEEDED

█ Not all the political-military organizations are included in the present National Coordinating Body (CN). Will it be open to the others?

"Yes, they certainly will be. In voicing our determination to move forward on an increasingly broad basis as regards uniting all the people, that means that the CN is open to other organizations. Moreover, by way of example: the unity agreement mentions the People's Revolutionary Army (ERP)....It is necessary for all the organizations to join forces for action against the common enemy....The people demand that....

"The creation of our coordinating body has had favorable repercussions among the masses and another body was founded from among them that includes the Popular Revolutionary Bloc, the 28th of February People's Leagues, the Unitary Popular Action Front and the Nationalist Democratic Union.

"It can be said that the coordination of the mass organizations represents a second stage, at the level of the fighting masses, the organized masses who are advanced in their awareness of the struggle and include large sectors of workers, peasants, middle strata and other groups of the population....

"However, there are other sectors of the people who should also become part of a process of rapprochement and unity. I refer to the democratic sectors of the Church, honest army officers, professionals and the small and middle-level business people; all those are included in the unity program.

"Of course, stages and channels must be established that will lead to the formation of a single bloc of unity, first on the basis of the political-military organizations, then the circle of militant popular mass organizations and finally the democratic organizations. Among the latter, I'm thinking, for instance, of the Social Democrats, the advanced sectors of the Christian Democrats. And naturally, the channels, bodies and links for unity have to be left open for those armed forces officers who are willing to fight alongside our people, in keeping with the interests of the working class and of working people in general.

"So, as can be objectively noted, we are at the start of a vast process of unity that will lead to the formation of broad revolutionary unity of the people, the basis for a people's revolutionary government."

CHRISTIAN DEMOCRATS

The United States is hastily supplying the present ruling junta in El Salvador with millions of dollars in emergency aid in an attempt to "stabilize" the revolutionary panorama that is jeopardizing its interests in Central America.

What is the role of the Christian Democrats in the Salvadorean regime?

Marcial, who in referring to the unity program included the "advanced" Christian Democrats, explained:

"After the collapse of the first ruling junta after less than two months in office, a second version is now on the scene, but in more difficult, precarious conditions, because U.S. imperialism has been forced to step in publicly, openly, barefacedly, to see just how it can shore up the Salvadorean regime.

"In addition to money, Washington has sent special officials who in talks with the Christian Democratic leaders got them to serve as a cover for the military dictatorship to continue to slaughter the people and intensify the counterrevolutionary war.

"The Christian Democrats lend themselves to all that, although let me point out that the Party is not monolithic. Three currents can be clearly distinguished.

"One of them is headed by José Napoleon Duarte, who has made a pact with the oligarchy and represents the most retrograde interests.

"In close alliance with the U.S. State Department is the sector headed by Ruben Zamora, who in the past claimed to be a left-winger but who now, in cooperation with the Duarte sector, represents what they themselves call the 'center to right.*'

"These two currents have isolated the most advanced sector of the Christian Democrats and brought about a 'new variation' which has no prospects, really, but does serve the interests of imperialism.

"Moreover, it is significant that the Christian Democratic reactionary turn preceded the appointment of the new U.S. ambassador, Mr. Robert White, who has served, no less, as adviser to the Stroessner dictatorship in Paraguay, one of the most monstrous regimes to plague a people of the Americas...."

INTERNATIONAL SOLIDARITY

In the case of Nicaragua, the support of the progressive peoples and governments of the world in general and of Latin America in particular prevented a direct military intervention.

How do you assess international solidarity?

"First of all, let me say that our people want to make their revolution in the framework of their legitimate right to self-determination. The United States has no right to meddle in El Salvador's economic, political or military affairs....Nevertheless, it seeks to maintain and bolster dependent capitalism at a point when our people feel the time has come to move on to other stages of struggle.

"Furthermore, we are certain that the solidarity of the anti-interventionist governments of the continent, as was the case with Nicaragua, will stop the bloodied fist of imperialism. We are also certain that our people will receive the powerful, determined support of all the peoples of the world who will do all they can to prevent any kind of armed intervention in El Salvador."

---

* Since the original Spanish publication of this interview, Ruben Zamora abandoned Duarte (December 1979) and formed with other progressive Christian Democrats the Social Christian Movement and joined the FDR.

EL SALVADOR: A GRAVE FOR THE MARINES

What about the possibility of direct U.S. armed intervention in El Salvador?

"It must be borne in mind that imperialism has prepared to intervene in Central America and the Caribbean, and it was evident that precisely when El Salvador became the scene of a real possibility for revolution, in September and October 1979, the president of the United States chose to stage that provocation around the lie about Soviet troops in Cuba....

"That gave Carter a pretext to get ready to intervene in our countries and that is the reason for the creation of the Rapid Deployment Force (RDF), ready to land in any country where the interests of the ruling classes and the imperialists are endangered....

"The United States has proclaimed its willingness to intervene in El Salvador and other Central American and Caribbean countries....Here it can do so with the puppet armies of Guatemala and Honduras and in the last analysis, it could use its own troops....If imperialism steps in directly, El Salvador will become another Vietnam and the grave of the marines."

NEAR FUTURE ONE OF GREAT STRUGGLES

What does the immediate future hold in store?

"The immediate future will be one of large-scale struggles for our people. The road to social liberation is not an easy one. We chose the course of prolonged people's war but this war, after ten years, is entering its final stages.

"Prolonged war does not mean interminable war. The accumulation of revolutionary elements throughout the process of the prolonged people's war, moving from the simple to the complex, has led to the war now entering the highest stages of the struggle....

"Our people's future is a future of victory of the revolution, and the building of a sovereign and independent state, and then the course towards higher stages of human coexistence, and we should not regard this as very remote in time."

From armed guerrillas to the Party

"ANA MARIA"

An extraordinary woman, "Ana Maria," holds the second highest post in the top leadership body of the Farabundo Martí Popular Liberation Forces (FPL).

Forty percent of the members of the Revolutionary Council, the leadership body of the political-military organization, are women.

Information of this kind can be revealed now by Prensa Latina because for the first time the Central Command invited a journalist to attend the final phase of what in essence was the recent Congress of the FPL, that is, the sixth meeting of the Revolutionary Council, which gathered together the most valuable, experienced and responsible cadres from all areas of work: organization, militia, guerrilla, army, mass organizations, finances, agitation and propaganda, etc. These are cadres tempered among the people, in the crucible of an intense struggle that does not see age as an obstacle.

The degree of women's participation in the leadership of the revolutionary war is especially surprising given the picture of social oppression, which is accentuated for the female half of the population.

In interviews conducted after the Council meeting - in a country where 80 percent of households have been destroyed - this writer was able to see for himself the decisive presence of women in the national military commission of the Central Command.

Prensa Latina, moreover, witnessed the dramatic death in battle in an attack on National Guard headquarters of 19-year-old "Patricia," a member of the guerrilla fighters' leadership in one zone in the country. Her unidentified body was taken by members of the repressive forces to a morgue, but that same night FPL members recovered the body and took it to a union office, where workers and others mounted a vigil to honor the young revolutionary.

The next day, Sunday, several thousand people staged an impressive demonstration of mourning as they walked to the cemetery following the workers and students who took turns carrying the coffin bearing the remains of Paula Emilia Osorio, "Patricia" in the underground.

"Eva," "Ursula," "Rumilia," "Juana Montano" are some of the women who preceded Paula Emilia along that same route.

Day after day, the struggle intensifies, the war spreads and takes on new dimensions.

The huge demonstration of 300,000 Salvadoreans in the capital on Tuesday, January 22, was attacked with unprecedented fury by the regular and paramilitary forces in the service of the fourteen families.

Fifty demonstrators were killed by bullets from the G-3s, while 230 others were wounded. However, the figure would have been much higher were it not for the self-defense mechanisms of the Farabundo Martí FPL, the National Resistance, the Communist Party and the People's Revolutionary Army (ERP), including a large number of women who fought intelligently and bravely to protect the people who are expressing their unconditional support for the unity of action agreement reached by the revolutionary and democratic forces.

The spirit of unity that prevails on the national scale can be measured by that courageous, extraordinary expression of the people's will on Tuesday, January 22. When 300,000 people decide to disregard the threats of mass murder to rally in a capital like San Salvador, with less than one million inhabitants, that means that the determination to stand together to speed up the demise of the present regime of social injustice is truly monolithic and unshakable.

Large numbers of women fighters in the guerrilla and militia forces took part in the preinsurrectional fighting from January 24 to 27 in Coatepeque and nine other cities and towns that were militarily occupied by the Farabundo Martí FPL. Some of the women were killed, and their names joined those of their comrade, Paula Emilia Osorio.

STRICT CLANDESTINITY

If the revolutionary war in El Salvador is difficult, complex and intense, the security measures surrounding the holding of a meeting lasting several days of the top body of the country's most important political-military revolutionary organization naturally had to be strict in the extreme.

At times this writer rode in the back of a vehicle enclosed in a sack. On other occasions, he had to keep his eyes closed and his head bent down. Sometimes, we had to hike long distances, following peasants along paths discreetly guarded by women and children. There were long hours of tension before we finally reached a place guarded by persons equipped with modern arms. Inside, everyone without exception was wearing the by now familiar hoods and masks.

The members of the Council and the journalist were not allowed to reveal their identities to one another. Only the top leader of the Farabundo Martí FPL, Salvador Cayetano Carpio, was authorized to disclose his.

A STRUCTURE OF ARMED COMMANDOS

The development of the Farabundo Martí FPL did not take place according to the classical principals that stress the need for a Party structure with political cells, on the basis of which the military bodies emerge.

In the case of the Salvadorean revolutionary organization, the starting point is a simple guerrilla structure that moves dialectically towards the complex, that is, in the direction of a class-conscious Party, and this generates a quantitative and qualitative leap in the struggle of the dispossessed masses.

At this point, we asked Carpio whether the roots of the FPL were to be found in the concept of the guerrilla foco.

"You have to remember that revolutionaries take objective reality and their knowledge of it as the point of departure for transforming it....And just what was our own reality?

"The initial group started virtually from zero. We lacked logistics, infrastructure, funds, arms and, if that weren't enough, we lacked military know-how. But at the same time, the people needed to be shown that on the strength of their own forces, they could and should take up arms against their enemies....So we had to choose between putting off the solution of that necessity and offering the people organizations that were incomplete and had already shown their inefficacy as all around means of struggle or else form armed commandos. We chose the latter course....

"An important element in that decision was the fact that most of us in the Farabundo Martí FPL were workers, people of working class origin. We'd led very militant workers struggles and had accumulated experiences and increased our awareness of the needs of the working class. We'd reached the conclusion that after so many years of military dictatorship, the electoral course was closed in our country and that the unions, in themselves, were not effective means for leading the people to liberation. We were convinced that the struggle limited to the political sphere, and especially to peaceful and legal means, was closed to our people....What we needed to do, then, was to get the people to trust their own ability to master other forms of struggle....Thus, instead of a Party structure, we began with the structure of armed commandos."

THE PEOPLE MAKE THE REVOLUTION

The man who knows the terrible depths of a society capped by a unified terror apparatus, who for over a year was held in secret jails in El Salvador where he was subjected to savage torture, the leader who day after day defies death alongside the dispossessed, the author of Secuestro y Capucha (Kidnapped and Hooded), that is, Comrade "Marcial" (Salvador Cayetano Carpio), stressed:

"After the years of struggle alongside the working class, we were thoroughly convinced that the people alone could make the revolution, and we were familiar with the enormous potential of the people, not only in theory but in practice....So, only if the Salvadorean people joined the struggle would it be possible to replace the society of exploitation with a better one, without exploited or exploiters....And so the armed commandos were the starting point....

"However, I should point out that from the start we regarded our line of action in terms of an all-around plan. The armed commandos, that is, the guerrillas, were never regarded as the absolute means to make the revolution, but simply as the primary bodies whose mission consisted of sounding a clarion to the people regarding the possibility of using other methods of struggle. At the same time, we reached out to the people to have them join both the armed struggle and other forms of popular struggle in which we are deeply involved....

"Thus, the first armed commandos were formed with the dialectical conception that they should at the same time reach out to the masses and work among them....

"Therefore, in just a few months' time, the political-military conception of the organization became an integral reality....To all appearances, then, if they weren't aware of our dialectical conception of the process, people could have thought that ours was a military plan.

"In a brief period of time, just a matter of months, our organization took shape as a military and political one - although in reality the dialectical concept was developing: the idea that the people alone could build their revolution and that, if we had to begin with guerrilla warfare, it was a passing stage, part of an overall plan that conceived the people as mastering all means and forms of struggle.

"That conception took us far away from the idea that the guerrilla on its own can make a revolution, that the guerrilla, isolated from the people, replaces the people in their prime tasks of carrying out their own transformation."

OUR OWN AND OTHER PEOPLE'S EXPERIENCES

In April, 1967, with El Salvador being ruled by a despotic military government, an unusual, revealing occurrence took place. Unity of action on the part of workers made possible a general strike declared in solidarity with the workers of Acero, S.A. steelworks, located two kilometers from Zacatecoluca, and which won for all the right to strike.

Salvador Cayetano Carpio, then leader of the Salvadorean bakery workers and one of the organizers of the strike, analyzed that moment in the history of the labor movement in a booklet called La Huelga General Obrera de Abril 1967 (The April 1967 General Workers Strike), which was recommended to the Central American workers for study.

Thirteen years later, he has this to say:

"In all honesty, we can state that, from the start, we ruled out the guerrilla foco theory....

"In that regard, we were helped a great deal by the experience of some guerrilla movements in South America and in other countries that were removed from the people, that failed to reach out to them to organize them and that succumbed to militaristic designs.... After building support groups, we attained a certain degree of influence among the working class and the student movement....However, our activity carried the most weight among the teachers....

"In 1974 we were able to reach out to the agricultural workers and the impoverished peasants. A lot of them joined our organization, which gave shape to the relation between the guerrilla and the mass movement as well as their mutual influence....This enabled us to steer clear of erroneous plans that we had witnessed in other revolutionary organizations...."

Carpio continued:

"Evidently, with the growth of our influence among the masses, a base began to arise for the development of the guerrillas, and, with the mounting militancy of the masses, a broad base for popular violence began to take shape that led to the setting up of mass self-defense corps and the people's militia....And, clearly, all this in turn helped to create the conditions and the need for a political vanguard organized as a party.

"Therefore, it would appear that we travelled unorthodox paths and arrived at a certain point that might seem should have been our starting point....But in fact, we set out to create the conditions which, in turn, created the Marxist working class party: with the masses, the guerrilla forces, the army, the militia, with a people in arms, a people in struggle for their immediate demands."

WE BEGAN WHERE WE HAD TO BEGIN

The leader of the Farabundo Martí FPL continued:

"The whole thing seemed to us a pretty simple application of dialectics: apparently we began backwards, but in fact we began where we had to begin, given the specific circumstances....Now we are building a growing Party with cadres who have been seasoned by the struggle: a Marxist-Leninist Party that leads the guerrilla, the militia, the army....The masses are joining....and the people, led by a vanguard, are taking the cause of the revolution into their own hands.

"Now, that seems to us to be Marxism, even though we started with armed commandos, because the implications are dialectical, and in the specific circumstances of our country, that was the most suitable course. We're not the only ones to have been through that experience: other organizations have also arisen in more or less similar circumstances."

FROM THE SIMPLE TO THE COMPLEX

"The experience of the Farabundo Martí FPL shows some interesting things. In the first place, we didn't formulate the guerrilla-or-Party problem in an artificial way - that is, what comes first? What has priority? - much less did we counterpose guerrilla and party. No, we didn't get tangled up in all those involved conflicts of the intellectuals, just as we didn't get bogged down in the armed struggle versus peaceful struggle dilemma....We dealt with objective reality in a clear-sighted way, from the simple to the complex, with an apparently unorthodox conception but one that is profoundly dialectical.

"And we felt that there was no reason to counterpose armed and political forms of struggle: rather, they had to be combined and promoted. The same can be said of the Party-guerrilla relation, since both belong to the development process of Salvadorean society, a dialectical process in which leadership naturally is in the hands of the revolutionary vanguard. And the same goes for the guerrilla-people, guerrilla-mass struggle relation: the whole is interrelated in such a way as to endow the process of social liberation with a faster pace.

"If we speak of combining all forms and means of struggle, if we believe in uniting, in rallying, why should we counterpose those means? The problem, as we've stressed, was the need for the people to master one more form of struggle but at a higher level, that is, armed struggle, and for the people to have confidence in their own forces....That was the reason for setting up the armed commandos....

"However, we began the difficult course with the conviction that only the people could transform society and hence needed to join an overall process on the basis of a political-military strategy, led by the working class in alliance with the peasants....

"The transition grows easier to the extent to which other classes, groups and sectors of society join the struggle. Our goal is the people's revolutionary alliance, whose strength and guarantee of continuity and development depend on the breadth and the correct leadership on the part of the working class Party, that guides the whole process, which includes the struggle of the mass organizations, the guerrilla, the militia, the army....From the struggle for immediate, basic demands to military combat.

"Thus, from the start, there has been ideological, political and military cohesion in the Farabundo Martí Popular Liberation Forces," the organization's top leader concluded.

The program of the Revolutionary Government

"The Popular Revolutionary Government (PRG), which will put an end to the rule by the fourteen families and the guardians of their wealth, and to imperialist plunder and oppression, will not be socialist," stated Salvador Cayetano Carpio, top leader of the Farabundo Martí Popular Liberation Forces (FPL), the organization whose political and military influence grows by the day in the country and heralds - in its unity of action with the National Resistance, the People's Revolutionary Army (ERP), and the Communist Party - the approach of the insurrectional stage and the inevitable end of the present regime of extreme social injustice.

The commander in chief of the Farabundo Martí FPL's militia, guerrilla forces and army, the designer and builder of a Party at war, explained to Prensa Latina that a government of workers and peasants alone would not be able to carry out the fundamental tasks of the essentially anti-imperialist, anti-oligarchic Salvadorean revolution.

"Those tasks are wide ranging and profound. In order to carry them out, cooperation is necessary, the determined and enthusiastic support of the broadest possible social sectors....That explains the need of a revolutionary popular alliance....an immense social base that

will guarantee freedoms and the broadest democracy....Present in that alliance, in addition to the
workers and the peasants, will be the small and middle
farmers and businessmen, the teachers, students,
employees, professionals, technicians and the priests
and military who are on the people's side....Thus, the
government will not be made up of one class alone -
although the workers in alliance with the peasants will
play the leading role - but rather it will be a government of all social sectors except the fourteen families,
the imperialists and their allies.... That means that we
too will be one of the forces comprising the vast
popular alliance."

IF THE FPL SAYS SO, IT MUST BE TRUE

A few years ago, in an attempt to cover up the
torturing and killing of political prisoners, the government of Colonel Arturo Armando Molina attempted to
trick the Salvadorean people and called into question
the seriousness and determination of the Farabundo
Martí FPL.

That was the first and only time, because the
mistake cost the oligarchy the life of Mauricio Borgonovo, Colonel Molina's foreign minister.

Since then no member of the fourteen families or
top official of the institutions at their service - much
less the representatives of foreign governments and
capital - has made any more mistakes regarding the
revolutionary political-military organization. And at
present it is hard to find people in El Salvador who
doubt or question the information supplied by the FPL.

"If the FPL says so, it must be true" has become a
saying in this country.

THE PHENOMENA OF CAUDILLISMO

The degree of development of the Farabundo Martí
Party is such that the "phenomena of caudillismo has
been overcome....Today any leader can fall in battle,
from the person in the top post to one of those holding
posts at lower levels, and our political-military organization would be in a position to replace that person
immediately," stated Salvador Cayetano Carpio.

A network of cells, "production," "geographical," and "special" cells built up during the development of the armed struggle and which is growing in breadth and depth, guarantees the continuity, leadership, organization, and coordination of the FPL.

The production cells constitute the fundamental basis of the Party and are located in places of work and study. The geographical cells answer to the need to organize, in terms of political-military strategy, hamlets, districts, neighborhoods, and big farms. The special cells function within the guerrilla forces and the rapidly growing Popular Liberation Army.

Thus the FPL Party is rooted in the people and directs, organizes and coordinates more easily vast social sectors in all spheres.

GOALS OF THE PEOPLE'S REVOLUTIONARY GOVERNMENT

Carpio stressed that the "Popular Revolutionary Government (PRG) will not be a socialist regime but will be a government which, with the efforts of all the people, will build the economy on the basis of independence and sovereign development...."

The objectives of the Salvadorean revolution, in its first stage and in keeping with the conception of the FPL, are, explains Comrade "Marcial," as follows:

"To put an end to domination by the imperialists and the fourteen families in the political, military, economic, cultural and social spheres.

"To transfer to the people the basic means of production that will make it possible to lay the groundwork for the transition to a new society: the large stretches of land, major means of transportation, electric power, the refineries, foreign trade - coffee, cotton, sugar, shrimp and others.

"To increase the overall standard of living of the population; promote the development of public health and education programs; create jobs; build housing; put an end to illiteracy; and do away with unemployment once and for all.

"To destroy the instruments of military and paramilitary oppression of the ruling classes by building the

People's Army in which all the officers of the old army who want to stand beside the people will have a place; to organize the masses, the people, at all levels and sectors; to build the organs of people's power; to conduct intense ideological work among the masses, especially among petty bourgeois sectors, so they can take their place alongside the workers and peasants to contribute to the construction and development of the revolutionary process that will lead to a new society.

"Of vital importance is the strengthening and defense of the revolutionary process....of a broad people's democracy....That is why the People's Revolutionary Government will rest upon the armed and organized people....only the people in arms can guarantee the advance of the process towards socialism.

"Those tasks and objectives will naturally be carried out in stages of a process which may be long or short, depending on the intensity of the efforts of the people and the leadership by the most advanced classes of our society."

THE PROGRAM

To destroy the power of the oligarchy and imperialism; to put the basic means of production in the hands of the Salvadorean people; to encourage and not damage the small and middle bourgeoisie; to guarantee a regime of democracy and freedoms, in a country where the capital city's radio and television stations ushered in the new year by playing the U.S. marines march; the People's Revolutionary Government will of necessity have to act firmly right from the start.

Salvador Cayetano Carpio says that the FPL feels that their program of the PRG should contain the following points:

"In the economic sphere, nationalize all the big companies with imperialist capital, including factories, banks, businesses and services; expropriate all the means of production in the hands of the fourteen families; centralize the planning of the economy; nationalize the banks; radically overhaul the tax system so workers are not obliged to pay taxes; nationalize the main public services - water, electricity, transportation, refineries, communications, ports and airports, large hotels and the like - carry out a thorough agrarian reform and lay the groundwork for urban reform; increase real wages through raises and price cuts on vital goods and services and state contributions to overall welfare - medicine, social security, vacations, etc. - establish mechanisms of aid and exchange among the small and middle property owners, who will benefit from a credit policy favorable to them.

"In the social sphere: free medical care; construction of hospitals and health care units in the rural and urban areas in keeping with population distribution; improvement of urban and intercity transportation services; creation of jobs that will eliminate unemployment and help fight the root causes of delinquency and other social problems; promotion of the broad organization of the workers, peasants and middle sectors in their respective unions and social, cultural, sports and other organizations....

"In the political and ideological sphere: the Legislative Assembly and the executive and judicial branches will be dissolved, as well as all government and state organs at the service of the oligarchy. A new Constitution will be drafted because the present one answers to the interests of imperialism, the fourteen families and their allies. The municipal government will be reorganized as so to ensure broad participation by the people. The main mass media will be nationalized. Elementary and secondary education will be made available to all children of school age, and illiteracy will be wiped out in two years at the most. The organization of the masses will be institutionalized: the people's power organs and bodies to defend the revolution will be set up. Relations will be established with all countries in the world, with priority assigned to relations with the progressive countries under the principles of mutual respect and self-determination. El Salvador will apply for membership in the Movement of Non-Aligned Countries....

"In the military sphere: the reactionary army will be dissolved at once and the People's Revolutionary Army set up, with the officers who are really on the people's side eligible for membership....

"At the same time the PRG will punish all those guilty of crimes against the people; it will dissolve the hated repressive bodies: the National Guard, the National Police, the Treasury Police, the Secret Police and ORDEN. El Salvador will leave the Central American Defense Council and other international bodies of the same type, created by imperialism to attack the oppressed peoples...."

The top leader of the FPL paused briefly before smiling confidently and declaring:

"Those requirements and measures are enough to get an idea of what the victory of the revolution will mean to the Salvadorean people. And that revolution is now at the higher stages of struggle that will be crowned by inevitable, conclusive victory."

Forging the Popular Armed Forces

"Precisely because the United States regards Latin America as its exclusive property and feels that it has the right to intervene directly whenever it decides that its interests and those of its partners are in jeopardy, the Popular Liberation Forces look upon the 'Central-Americanization' of the revolutionary struggle as a key part of their strategy to confront imperialism," explains "Isabel," one of the many women who have taken up arms in this oppressed "Tom Thumb" of Latin America. However, there is something that distinguishes "Isabel" from other women: she is a member of the top body that directs the work and military operations of the Farabundo Martí FPL, whose commander in chief is Salvador Cayetano Carpio, the best known leader of the Salvadorean working class.

With the approach of the decisive moment of insurrection conducted by a people with the necessary awareness, courage and determination to be free, the United States' presence grows increasingly patent and the repression sharpens. The fascist ORDEN gangs broke into the home of Attorney General of the Republic Mario Zamora Rivas and killed him with machine gun blasts. They kidnapped Juan Chacón, general secretary of the Popular Revolutionary Bloc (BPR), his wife and their infant daughter, and Carlos Argueta, leader of the 28th of February Popular Leagues. They blew up the Catholic Church's radio station and the Jesuits' publishing house. In broad daylight, on one of San Salvador's main thoroughfares, they murdered leaders of the General Association of University Students. They kidnap, torture and kill young women and men suspected of belonging to revolutionary political-military organizations. They threatened Archbishop Oscar Arnulfo Romero with death many times and implacably hunt priests José Rutilio Sánchez and José David Gutiérrez.

International solidarity is urgently needed for a people whose will to unite, multiply and rally their forces is greater than ever before in the face of threats from abroad.

"The United States has never asked permission to invade Latin America....The time has come for all our peoples to close ranks before the main enemy....The revolution in Central America is one and indivisible, and the Salvadorean process cannot and must not be regarded in an isolated fashion, separate from the struggle unfolding in Guatemala and Honduras," declared "Camilio," another member of the National Military Commission of the Farabundo Martí Popular Liberation Forces.

CENTRAL AMERICA: A REVOLUTIONARY FLASH POINT

The United States is rushing arms shipments and advisors to El Salvador. At the U.S. military bases in Panama, specialized counterinsurgency troops are conducting intensive exercises, while in Guatemala and Honduras military movements are taking place with their sights trained on the Salvadorean revolutionary process.

The elite divisions that were recently set up by the Carter administration for use in "cases of emergency" are stationed in the Caribbean, awaiting the order to intervene.

 What are the prospects for revolution in Central America?

"Isabel" replied:

"The picture is clear. In Guatemala, the people are resisting and have taken up arms against the opprobious military dictatorship headed by General Romero Lucas García. The Guerrilla Army of the Poor (EGP), the Organization of the People in Arms (ORPA), the Revolutionary Armed Forces (FAR), the Guatemalan Party of Labor (PGT) and labor organizations provide an example of struggle in Latin America....In Honduras, the Francisco Morazán National Liberation Front (named after the outstanding architect of Central American unity in the 19th century - T.N.), the Communist Party and the mass organizations fight for a new society with social justice....

"In the sister Republic of Costa Rica, the Popular Vanguard and Socialist Parties, the Popular Revolutionary Movement and the Revolutionary Workers Movement-II are mass organizations which in the national and Central American framework struggle and provide solidarity to the peoples of the area.... In Panama, a deeply anti-imperialist people are the object of pressures by U.S. imperialism, because they are fighting for their genuine sovereignty and independence.

"Here in El Salvador, the unity of action of the revolutionary and democratic forces is an extraordinary step that brings us close to victory....The Farabundo Martí FPL supports all moves that effectively mean relief for the working people of our own country and of Central America....And we will continue to fight to set up a people's revolutionary government working towards socialism. This mighty struggle in the area, especially since the victory of the people in Nicaragua, has turned Central America into a genuine revolutionary flash point with a main enemy: U.S. imperialism....Hence, our organization defines the Central-Americanization of the struggle as a fundamental part of its strategy."

THE POPULAR LIBERATION ARMY

Who belongs to the Popular Liberation Army (EPL)? What development stage has it reached, and what are its goals?

The National Military Commission of the Farabundo Martí FPL, set up in 1975, informed the following to El Salvador and the world for the first time, in this interview with Prensa Latina:

"The combatants of the Popular Liberation Army are farmers, farm workers, industrial workers, students, teachers, and women and men of other social sectors who, imbued with a great love for the people and sensitive to their sufferings and the abuse they're subjected to, are prepared to give their own lives to attain a better world. The EPL's goal is the destruction of the strategic military forces of the fourteen families and imperialism. It is developing a mobile war. Today it has demonstrated its capacity to strike against the enemy throughout the country.

"It is preparing, along with the rest of the Salvadorean people, to wage the great decisive battles for taking power....The EPL fights against the army of the oligarchy with the power of the arms of the people and their military organization, and, in the victorious future, will guarantee the building of the economic, political and social bases of a new government that will promote the people's welfare....This is a people's armed force arising from the impoverished, exploited masses which, in the heat of the daily battle, has been taking on greater strength and forming regular military units that will contribute, in the military sphere, to putting a people's government in power...."

What is the organizational structure of the EPL and the guerrilla forces of the Farabundo Martí FPL?

"Camilio" replied this time:
"You must remember that the units of the EPL have a strategic nature, they are mobile, nationwide and centralized, while the guerrilla units operate in a specific zone, with the mission of supporting the actions of the EPL through permanent harassment and softening up the enemy on his territorial base. The Farabundo Martí guerrillas live clandestinely in the midst of the people, as full-time fighters. The people

are their eyes and ears. They operate only in the zone assigned to them and they surface, attack and fall back with speed....Their military activity is limited to a certain zone, but that doesn't mean that they live there....Generally, the guerrillas live in one zone and operate in another, where the local militia, which channels the revolutionary violence of the masses, provides them with the necessary support for attaining the political-military objective....

"Both in the guerrilla forces and the EPL, the basic unit is the point of departure. This unit is the squad, followed by the platoon, section, detachments and general staffs, which in the case of the guerrilla are zonal and in that of the EPL, national. Both come under the National Military Commission of the Central Command."

THE REAR GUARD: THE PEOPLE

Whenever a revolutionary movement shows notable tactical-operational capacity of a military nature and checks the forces that protect a system of social injustice, those whose interests are seriously harmed or threatened claim that the insurgents receive arms, training and funds from abroad. El Salvador could hardly have been exempted, much less in the case of the Farabundo Martí Popular Liberation Forces, the most important political-military organization in the country.

Where do the Salvadorean fighters train and from where do they get arms and funds?

"Camilio" was about to answer, but a smile that "Isabel's" hood failed to hide neutralized her fellow-member of the National Military Commission, and she replied:

"At first it might seem hard to understand the whole matter of arms, training, and funds, but remember, our country has been ruled by a military dictatorship for close to half a century. In fact, our 'military training' begins when we're children, in the street, in daily 'combat' against the repressive bodies. First you throw stones, then you develop the most important thing, the thing that the exploiters just can't understand: revolutionary consciousness and a fighting spirit.

"The Salvadorean people's heroism is indescribable, and the people, at a later stage, provided us with the protection required to set up our training camps. The enemy can be 20 meters from a training center, yet he doesn't find it. He can organize combing operations, from La Union, in the east, to Santa Ana, in the west, and never come upon a single of our training camps.

"He doesn't find the camps because our people are with the revolution and know how to protect their fights....Moreover, since the members of the Popular Liberation Army and the guerrilla forces are immersed in the people, who suffer the criminal repression of military operations against entire villages - Aguilares, Cinquera, San Pedro Perulapán, to mention a few examples - where people are murdered indiscriminately, these painful experiences of war oblige the revolutionary combatants to develop and perfect an infinite number of variations of military tactics, a mastery that later on enables us to strike more efficiently against the enemy forces....The repression also motivates the Salvadorean people to supply invaluable aid in foodstuffs, information and guidance in our movements that enables us to steer clear of ambushes on highways and side roads....

"So you see, the unbeatable rear guard of the EPL, the 'mountain retreat' where the EPL fighters find a secure haven, is the Salvadorean people, and their revolutionary consciousness is the indestructible machine gun whose caliber is produced only by the masses for annihilating the regular and irregular troops of those who are immensely rich thanks to the hunger, the blood and the labor of the dispossessed. In addition, we seize our weapons from the enemy. They are the same arms that the United States, the North Atlantic Treaty Organization, Israel and South Africa supply to the Salvadorean military. Our funds come from expropriations and the capture of oligarchs in exchange for whose release we obtain an infinitesimal portion of the surplus value they steal from the workers."

How come there are no military ranks in the EPL, the guerrilla forces and the militia?

"Military ranks," replies "Camilo," "are limited to the chiefs of platoons, squads, sections, detachments. The only title is that of commander in chief, that is, the rank of Comrade "Marcial" (Salvador Cayetano Carpio), because we feel that at this stage our members need to be filled with the revolutionary creed; they must acquire a proletarian way of thinking and keep in mind that all that interests us is the welfare of the masses and that our lives are at the service of the people....We don't think that at this stage of the process calling a comrade captain or commander helps any.... The important thing is not what we call our leaders, but why they are leaders, and what they do in our people's struggle...."

ON KIDNAPPING

The revolutionary movement frequently uses kidnapping as a weapon in the struggle for the transformation of Salvadorean society, a weapon that is argued about from the ethical angle and which raises doubts among some social sectors.

What are the objectives sought with kidnapping?

"Isabel" replied:

"Kidnapping is a political, economic and military weapon that the workers and the people in general use to defend their interests. It is a tool that helps the revolutionaries attain certain objectives which otherwise would be impossible or very difficult to bring about. Kidnapping from this standpoint can have economic, political, and military objectives. Economic, because a portion of the surplus value stolen from our working people is recovered to serve the interests of the masses in the process of social liberation instead of financing the vices of the fourteen families....For instance, the funds are earmarked for the families of comrades who have disappeared or are dead, the sustenance of our full-time, professional revolutionaries, the purchase of arms....and other aims that are part of the anti-imperialist, anti-oligarchical revolution.

"You should see how the Salvadorean bourgeoisie fights wage increases for the workers....Now, it's perfectly true that our political-military organization is supported by the masses, who contribute funds and other means for the struggle. However, it is obvious that a people like the Salvadoreans, who are poverty-striken because of overexploitation, need to find ways to recover from the exploiters funds for promoting the revolutionary struggle.

"It is very hard for people to spare much out of their starvation wages. To be sure, when people have an omelet they give us half of it and this intensifies our commitment still further. As for the destination of the funds we obtain, the organization keeps detailed accounts of all that is spent. The destination is one, the revolution....

"From the political standpoint, kidnapping serves to draw attention to the plight of the Salvadorean people and the reasons for their struggle....In exchange for the life of an oligarch, the government is forced to authorize the publication, inside the country and abroad, of full-page communiques reporting on the situation in our country and the demands made by our organization, demands which the government may or may not meet, but which denounce it in one way or another....

"A revealing example was the case of oligarch Mauricio Borgonovo Pohl, the foreign minister....The main condition for his release was for General Carlos Humberto Romero to present to the people and release a certain number of political prisoners....The aims of that kidnapping were to rescue revolutionary cadres in order to promote our people's process of struggle and put an end to the grief of hundreds of relatives....The government was unable to meet our demands because several of the comrades had died under torture. The people found out about the crimes committed, and progressive persons who were serving in the regime of Romero because they were unaware of the workings of the official terror machinery at once condemned it and approved our action.

"Kidnapping as a political objective also allows us at a given moment to express our solidarity with the struggles of other peoples and at the same time denounce some specific imperialist maneuver. That was the case with South African Ambassador Archibald Gardner Dunn. We Salvadoreans feel deep love and enthusiasm for the struggle of the peoples of South Africa, Namibia, Rhodesia and Palestine against racism and apartheid, against colonialism, neocolonialism and Zionism and for national independence and peace....

"In addition to publicizing a revolutionary message of solidarity with the blacks and Palestinians, we called attention to the maneuver imperialism was conducting at the time concerning the first ruling junta in El Salvador (after the overthrow of Romero in October 1979). That junta was depicted as democratic and progressive outside the country, while here at home it was extremely repressive and criminal....However, our demands were not met....Our organization is consistent with its formulations and has never given its word on anything that it has failed to carry out. For instance, if we say that a certain oligarch will be released if given conditions are met, if those conditions are not met, we do not demand new ones. Revolutionary struggle must earn the respect of both the people and the enemy, who is obliged to recognize - and does recognize - the seriousness of the Farabundo Martí FPL.

"And another thing: look at the difference between the treatment received by an oligarch in a people's prison and that meted out to a revolutionary in a dungeon or torture chamber of a secret jail of the National Guard or some other repressive body. We take care of our prisoner's health, cleanliness, emotional state. He is given books and, despite the circumstances, we try to make his life bearable.

"From the military standpoint, kidnapping enables us to obtain information that permits us to act against strategic objectives of the enemy or against war criminals. And in this regard, trials will begin very shortly.

"When a kidnapping is conducted, the organization takes responsibility for the person held in the people's prison and we communicate the action and our demands to the family. Since the kidnapping is political, the negotiations are always conducted publicly. The Farabundo Martí Popular Liberation Forces never act with their backs to the masses."

Creating the conditions
for local armed insurrections

The occupation of four cities and the same number of villages and two large urban districts, in addition to hamlets; plus hard-hitting attacks on garrisons and ambushes of National Guard and army convoys throughout the country indicate that the Farabundo Martí Popular Liberation Forces have launched their political-military offensive "to pave the way for popular insurrection."

For the first time since they were set up in 1976, numerous militia columns and brigades went into action, clad in olive green uniforms, their faces partly covered by red bandannas, their caps with their organization's insignia and automatic rifles or light machine guns in hand. The militia operated alongside the guerrillas and in a 72-hour period, they occupied the following:

■ The cities of Coatepeque, 15,000 inhabitants, in Santa Ana department, in the western part of the country; Tenancingo, 10,000 people, Cabañas department, in the center-north; Santa Elena, 10,000 people, in the eastern department of Usulután; and Santa Clara, 6,000 people, in San Vicente department, in what is known as the "para-central" region.

■ The villages (3,000-4,000 inhabitants) of Tejutla, El Jícaro, and Los Mangos, in the northern department of Chalatenango; and Monte San Juan, in Cuscatlán, in the center;

■ The districts (3,000) people of La Periquera in Santa Ana and La Curruncha, in the eastern department of San Miguel.

At the same time, the growing Popular Liberation Army, of the Farabundo Martí FPL, wiped out the troops of the garrisons of Agua Caliente and Tejutla, in the Chalatenango; staged harassment attacks on the police stations in Zacamil in San Salvador, and Occidente, in Santa Ana; staged an ambush of a military convoy of 150 soldiers on the northern highway to Tutultepeque, between Aguilares and Suchitoto; and carried out another ambush in Cinquera, Cabañas department, against two National Guard patrols.

Thus, in a matter of hours, the Farabundo Martí FPL put into practice several different kinds of military operations that produced close to 100 casualties among the guardians of wealth of the oligarchy. They obtained large numbers of arms, gave political and military instruction to the people gathered in the public squares where, in addition, the local cutthroats were tried and then punished in keeping with the sentences handed down by the people. They bolstered the people's self-defense bodies and gave a rundown of the national situation, ending with an appeal to the Salvadoreans present to join the armed struggle, an invitation accepted by a good number of people between Thursday, January 24 and Sunday, January 27.

These pre-insurrectional actions pointed up the two fundamental aspects of the FPL's political-military strategy for taking power:

1) Popular armed insurrection, proceeding always from the simple to the complex, that is, beginning with local and then regional insurrection and concluding with the general insurrection;

2) Surprise attacks on the forces of the oligarchy in movement or in their barracks, by the Popular Liberation Army.

POPULAR LIBERATION MILITIA

Somewhere in this nation at war, where the writer witnessed actions carried out by the three branches of the Popular Liberation Armed Forces - militia, guerrilla, army - we interviewed the national leadership of the militia, which is in practice the people's armed instrument par excellence.

"Antonio," "Ramiro" and "Maria" replied to Prensa Latina's questions:

▓ What is the militia and how does it operate?

"The militia is the paramilitary instrument that the FPL uses to lead the people in self-defense, as regards the violence of the masses and armed insurrection....It is made up of people from all social sectors, mainly workers and peasants and other persons involved in production....The militia is a local organization, because its members, that is, those who carry out armed actions at a higher level, operate in the area where they work. The link with production is decisive....That's why the militia doesn't move around geographically speaking....Its activities take the form of street fighting, of the self-defense of the masses. It directs the people's violence in armed actions, and also has guerrilla-type military operational ability which consists of actions of armed propaganda and sabotage....In addition, the militia takes charge of punishing the enemies of the people, in keeping with the demands of the people."

▓ What is the difference between the militia, the guerrilla and the army?

"In the first place, as we've said, the militia is to be found in the factories, the fields, the schools - that is, wherever people work and study - naturally in the strictest underground conditions....The members of the militia are engaged in production, they do not leave their daily tasks....That's why the militia is local and lacks mobility. Only the leadership cadres of the militia are full-time professionals....The army and the guerrilla, however, are comprised of full-time, professional fighters....They devote themselves to the development of military skills to promote armed struggle. The mobility of the guerrilla is limited to a given zone.... The army has nationwide mobility and goes wherever the fighting needs to be stepped up....In addition, the techniques and the weapons of the army and the guerrilla are different from those of the militia, in keeping with the activities conducted by each branch...."

How is the militia organized?

"You must keep in mind that the people's militia is a mass organization, that is, thousands of the most advanced working people belong to it....

"Its structure can be analyzed at three levels: the grassroots combat units, each of which is made up of four to six members; the brigade, comprised of two to four grassroots units, or, to put it another way, a brigade, including its chiefs, may have up to 26 combatants; and finally, the column, comprised of two or three brigades with a maximum of 80 members counting the tactical officers of the smaller units.

"Politically and militarily, the militia column comes under the leadership of the locality, because the militia is structured on a local basis. Several of these in turn come under a leadership level known as municipal, although the 'municipality' here does not coincide with the official government divisions....A given group of municipalities comes under a subzone leadership. All the foregoing can be summed up as follows: a subzone is divided into several municipalities, each of which has its own leadership. The municipality in turn is divided into localities with their leadership, while each locality is organized into columns, brigades and grassroots combat units.

"A group of subzones makes up a zone, under a zone general staff, while these staffs are centralized and unified by the national general staff of the militia, which directs and coordinates and synchronizes the operations and activities and the militia movement in general....

"A body above the national general staff of the militia is now being organized, namely, the joint general staff of the Popular Liberation Armed Forces, which politically and militarily will lead the militia, the guerrilla forces and the army.

"At the very top is the supreme command, which is, at the same time, the central command of the Farabundo Martí FPL....Hence, at the top, the political-military leadership of the vanguard merges - or, what amounts to the same thing, becomes the Party - with the leadership of its military bodies....

"It should be stressed that the functioning of the militia, from the grassroots unit right up to the national general staff, is clandestine, because, were this not the case, at this stage of the war, not to speak of the early days, the comrades would be risking their lives as well as endangering the organization of the militia.

"The people know the militia members are present and act in defense of their interests, but they don't know their identity....In all combative actions of the masses, and not only in military operations, the masses are accompanied by grassroots militia units: in mobilizations, in the occupation of lands, factories, public buildings, etc. The militia members merge with the popular defense bodies (the security commissions) from which they guide and promote the militancy of the masses. That's why when a demonstration is attacked by regular and irregular forces at the service of the oligarchy and its allies, the Salvadorean people know how and to where they must withdraw, while their self-defense bodies put a brake on the aggressors' movements. The militia is a political body of a paramilitary nature located within the masses."

ARMS AND TRAINING

Outside El Salvador there is speculation on the origin of the arms used by the FPL. Just where do the militia get their weapons?

"Basically the arms of the militia come from the enemy, from whom we seize them through military actions....Many of the weapons we possess today belonged to criminals who are members of the reactionary para-military bodies at the local level....Moreover, the Salvadorean people collaborate by supplying arms to the militia. You might have seen some examples during the occupation of a city or village. People figure that these arms are put to better use in our hands. But the militia also uses homemade weapons such as grenades, bombs, and mines. You can be sure that the large-scale produc-tion of weapons is well organized. Aside from that, people's ingenuity knows no bounds. They come up with all kinds of traps to be used on the roads leading into our organized zones...

"The oligarchy and its allies are well aware that today attacking our people is not so easy, because the people know how to fight back."

At first glance, one might think that the topography of El Salvador, the lack of high mountains, the abun-dance of roads, and the high population density are obstacles for training and furthering the militia organ-ization.

■ How do you get around those obstacles?

"Those obstacles are part of our objective real-ity....That is a fact, but another fact is that the militia draws from an extraordinarily rich reality: the mili-tant, organized people of El Salvador, who are at the service of the revolution and who want their social liberation....So the people's talent and determination help overcome the obstacles....Moreover, those obsta-cles really spur people on. Thanks to the people, militia training schools have been set up at different levels, the grassroots combat units, the brigades, the columns.

"These training centers, which are organized at the zone level, are mobile, they have no fixed place....They arise when the opportunity presents itself and disappear when circumstances so require. Ultimately, it's the people who decide when and where. Now, that goes for the training of the militia. But military instruction is also provided to the self-defense bodies of the masses and to the population at large....Each time we occupy a city, a village or a rural hamlet, the local people are given military instruction, since one of our objectives is setting up a military reserve among the civilian population to prepare for the armed insurrection and to bolster the people's military units....

"Moreover, since the militia members as such are clandestine, they continue as workers, and those with the greatest experience are chosen to provide instruction to small, secret groups. There is even training in specialized subjects.

"We take advantage of every possible opportunity to further our people's political-military knowledge, but without falling into the trap of spontaneity nor violating the rules of underground life...."

LOCAL INSURRECTION IN 1980

What do you have to say about this year, which has begun with actions of a pre-insurrectional nature?

"We will concentrate our efforts against the repressive forces on local armed insurrections, on blows by the guerrilla forces and the growing Popular Liberation Army. We are attempting to develop the political-military instruments of the Salvadorean people, in order to achieve leaps in quality and win social liberation."

Intellectuals incorporate themselves into the armed struggle

SALVADOR
SAMAYOA

"I've had time to think about things a lot more....I made the right choice....and I think that any sacrifice I may have to make will be made with hope and optimism," Salvador Samayoa*, minister of education in the first government junta after the ouster of General Carlos Humberto Romero in October 1979, told Prensa Latina in the strictest underground conditions.

This writer also interviewed him before his resignation on January 2 and his surprise announcement six days later that he was joining the Farabundo Martí Popular Liberation Forces, made at the law school of the National University in a crowded auditorium occupied militarily by members of the Farabundo Martí FPL. In the present, exclusive interview, the 29-year-old philosophy graduate stressed: "There is no power in the world, no matter how great, that can defeat an entire people determined to win their freedom."

A model student of the Jesuit priests at the Central American Catholic University, where he later became a member of the faculty, Samayoa held the education portfolio for 73 days. His decision to join the FPL was a bombshell for the Salvadorean intellectuals and other liberal sectors, which he now urges to "live with the people and feel, in the heat of combat, the correctness of their struggle...."

---

* Salvador Samayoa is presently one of the members of the 7-member Political-Diplomatic Commission of the FDR/FMLN.

This writer interviewed a new Samayoa. Physically and spiritually he was transformed. The interview follows:

How do you feel about your new life as a member of the Farabundo Martí FPL?

"The first thing I should point out about my new life is something I'd imagined but really hadn't experienced in practice: the great degree of comradeship that I've found in all my comrades in work and struggle....From the human standpoint, the reception I've been given has helped me a great deal....The conditions are difficult....

"It means a radical change in your whole life-style, big things and little things that you're used to or which, through routine, have shaped you. It involves certain difficulties and privations, constant risk and certain duties at a fairly high level. That is, you must be prepared to give your life at any time, because any clash, especially in a case like mine, could mean that the most repressive sectors of the ruling classes and the army would be even more savage in an attempt to show certain sectors that my choice was incorrect and that the power of the repressive apparatus is so great that they can always find such cases....So, the sacrifice really is a big one, and I feel that it can be made only through the experience, the degree of hope, commitment and generosity of all the comrades....Without that it would be very hard to adopt a life-style involving so many privations, risks and sacrifices....But when you're constantly sharing the hope of a more just society and also sharing the high degree of discipline and commitment with your comrades, it encourages you, it's an incentive that cannot be appreciated abstractly, from the outside....

"Perhaps, at first, it's an act of faith, with a certain objective basis. Later, in daily life, you realize just how much it is worth....So I'm really happy about my choice. I've thought about it a lot more....I feel I made the right choice - without a doubt....I think that any sacrifice I may have to make will be made with hope and optimism....And this should not be regarded as an emotional decision....I truly feel the heat of the struggle. I feel that we are at a higher stage, and I think that the interval before final victory for the people may well be shorter than some think."

AN OBJECTIVE NEED FOR ARMED STRUGGLE

▌▌▌ Why did you choose this course?

"I think the key factor was coming to the full realization that the regular army of El Salvador is utterly pledged to defend always the interests of the oligarchy by force....

"I see no way for the people to be able to confront that solid military apparatus without another equally or more solid military apparatus....I don't see how any other instruments of struggle can produce positive results in this country, where for the past 30 years they have been tried, in very different ways and under different guidelines, and the result has always been a progressive deterioration of the living conditions of the people, the progressive deterioration of the economic model and, moreover, an increasingly firm determination on the part of the oligarchy and its repressive forces to wipe out, to exterminate, the popular organizations....

"The choice of armed struggle is in keeping with an absolutely objective necessity given El Salvador's present-day situation and background. The masses must create their own revolutionary instruments of self-defense and resistance at a given time, and then move from self-defense to the taking of power. I just don't see how you can stand up to a military power unless it is with another military power...."

POLITICAL AND HUMAN CONSIDERATIONS

▌▌▌ What led you to join the Farabundo Martí FPL?

"To me, that is the heart of the matter....I've said before that I felt a greater political affinity with the Farabundo Martí FPL....perhaps because, as a university teacher, I've always been concerned with following the political lines - both theoretical and in practice - of the different trends the popular movement has followed, concretely, the revolutionary movement....And it seems to me that, so far, the organization with the most coherent, solid and consistent line for combining the different revolutionary instruments and the armed struggle with the mass movement is precisely the FPL.

"I think the falsity of the guerrilla foco theory has been demonstrated. An armed struggle that is not deeply rooted in the people and which fails to continuously generate and encourage the development of the mass movement, the mass front, is doomed to failure from the start....In terms of that line of setting up broad mass fronts in all sectors - workers, peasants, students, teachers, etc. - I think that it is objectively proven that the FPL has displayed greater political clarity since its inception.

"In addition, I believe it is also moving with greater clarity....in the direction of a genuine Party of the Salvadorean revolution....I think that without the organizational solidness of a Party, no group or organization can become the vanguard of the popular movement.... Actually, it must demonstrate in practice, with actual facts, that it possesses sufficient organization, political and military consolidation, to then seek to become the vanguard of the masses.

"Anything else would amount to a fraud or a pipe-dream....The FPL, it seems to me, has been extremely serious in this regard. From the start, even before it went public with a name, it spent nearly two years working and fighting beginning in 1970....The easy thing, the usual practice, is for any group to declare itself the revolutionary vanguard or the Party of the revolution without any objective basis....So, in this regard, I say that politically the organization of the FPL has always seemed to me more solid, more complete as a revolutionary method, and more consistent in following its principles, purer - so pure that lots of people probably criticize the FPL for being inflexible or rigid, but I regard this as a very important point: its closeness to the masses and its clearsightedness about the kind of organization that needs to be built up at the different stages....

"I believe that so far the results are quite clear. There are weaknesses, but unquestionably the organization has become impressively strengthened over the past ten years, at the cost of many sacrifices, and thanks to a great deal of clear-sightedness and consistency in following principles.

"As for political closeness to the masses, people often get the idea - and this is the result of systematic smear campaigns in the mass media - that the FPL is just a guerrilla force....engaging in armed actions and lacking in wholeness as a revolutionary organization....That is utterly false. I regard armed struggle, or the armed method of struggle, as an objective need of our people, in the present conditions. Our organization carries out integral political-military work.... This means a lot. It means serious and solid political training of cadres; hard work on organizational questions; international work; work to raise, in integral fashion, the consciousness and the standard of living of the masses and their political life....

"It isn't just conducting the armed actions. In that regard, because the FPL had a more complete line, I felt closer to it....In regard to the human factor, I feel it is a mistake, or a danger, that has been evidenced, unfortunately, in many past experiences and on a world-wide scale, for a given movement to begin to forge a new man, the new society, free of injustice and oppression, at the moment of taking power. I think this is impossible unless, during the process of political-military struggle, the members of the organization have already become new people, unless, during the struggle, the organization's life-style involves new social relations....It's not that I underestimate the members of other organizations, but I believe that the members of the FPL are more advanced in the overall human aspect and in the revolutionary line....That is, we aren't waiting to take power to do those things. That would be inconsistent....

"Here, in the underground of the FPL, I have felt the extremely high degree of comradeship, friendship....discipline, sacrifice, devotion and respect for all the human values that capitalism and the bourgeoisie have deformed....In this organization people live with these values and I feel that they are the basis upon which it has been able to survive under such difficult conditions and has been able to grow and develop, and attract many sectors of the people with such intensity....From that standpoint, I feel that all the comrades with whom I've had the opportunity to work or converse already reflect or embody, to a considerable degree, the values of the new man and the new society that we want to build in El Salvador."

UNITY IS ESSENTIAL

What do you think about the unity of the revolutionary forces in El Salvador?

"Unity is the necessary condition for carrying forward the revolutionary process. I think that we've reached a stage of struggle that is at such a high level and is so polarized....that the enemy onslaught will soon take the shape of an all-out, open offensive.... Counterinsurgency warfare, without any cloak or cover, is about to be waged....And if at that time the revolutionary forces are not united militarily, politically and organizationally, none of them on their own will be able to withstand all-out, open attack by the enemies of the people....

"Thus, unity is needed and the revolutionary organizations know this....The first step has been taken.... Naturally, there will be difficulties because, as I said before, I think that the political-military organizations have for years acted in response to different formulations and guidelines....and it isn't going to be easy to unify some things....Practice has shown the historical validity of some guidelines and principles over others, and I regard political modesty as a virtue that all genuine revolutionary organizations and members of them possess....You can't set out to defend something that is not in keeping with the objective results. So, from the standpoint of principles, there will be fewer problems....

"Difficulties may arise in regard to work methods or organizational matters, especially because in El Salvador the conditions of struggle and for building that kind of organization are extremely difficult....We are forced to act in virtually complete underground conditions. We have no mountains as a physical rearguard; the people are our mountains, and that has its advantages but also its limitations, since we do not possess the ideal conditions for carrying out integration....of different lines....

"However, such a clear awareness exists of the need for unity and of the meaning of this political moment for the country, that all differences will have to be overcome....for the sake of the people....The idea is not for one organization to dominate the struggle; rather, a political line must dominate the struggle, and that is quite a different matter....That line must be clearly proletarian and absolutely honest and consistent with all its principles....So, I hail this first step towards unity....which is absolutely necessary....It shows the degree of political maturity attained by our organizations and ultimately by the masses of this country."

JOIN THE STRUGGLE

What message do you have for the circles you moved in for several years?

"The opportunity Prensa Latina is giving me is important, because at this time we need to pool all our efforts....In the first place, I feel that the most liberal academic and intellectual petit bourgeois sectors, which is where I come from, have committed the very serious mistake of, in practice, having our backs to the popular movement. We've committed the error of failing to learn to share the people's lives and feel in the heat of struggle the correctness of their principles and their methods. We have made the mistake of trying to set forth, on the basis of theoretical conceptions, what the form, modality and stages of the struggle should be, without appreciating the elements you can grasp only when you're really inside the struggle, with the people. Statements of intention aren't enough....

"This is the first message I'd send to all the comrades in whom I found great human, political and intellectual qualities....I think they need to place all their knowledge, vitality and sensitivity at the service of the struggle and the popular movement, not in the abstract but through its concrete revolutionary instruments. It is possible - in fact, it's certain - that those revolutionary instruments have their weaknesses, but what we must not and cannot do is fall upon those weaknesses with the full weight of the theoretical critical apparatus, from outside....What we need to do is attempt to overcome those weaknesses from within, by joining the popular struggle ourselves....

"It's the most normal thing in the world for a political line that has consistently been a proletarian, mass line to display certain weaknesses in some areas, along with its great wealth, but then, what we as intellectuals should do, concretely, is join the people, stand with the people. We need to realize that we have a lot to learn from the people in struggle, and we also need to realize that we have a great deal to contribute, but from within....

"In the second place, I'd like to alert my fellow university professors, and also my own teachers and other similar circles to keep open and critical minds in the face of the bourgeois press and propaganda machine's constant campaigns to discredit the people's political-military organizations. I'd especially like to tell them, given the bourgeois way of presenting the revolutionary organizations, that the most natural thing - and this is something I felt myself in those circles - is for them to feel an aversion to the political work carried out by those revolutionary organizations....Given this situation I feel that we should seek direct contact with the popular movement and with the people: the peasants, the workers, with their organizations, to get to know them instead of relying on the criteria that come from other sectors with an ulterior motive, which is to wipe out the popular movement....

"My message is for there to be a desire to join the struggle; that there be political will to join the popular struggle; that people be modest enough to realize that there is something to be learned and something to be contributed; and that there must be political clear-sightedness to realize that this is a higher phase of struggle; that we may well enter the final stretch before long; that this is a highly polarized process, class structure and form of struggle, in which the middle of the road doesn't exist: either you're with the people, with their instruments; or you're going to turn increasingly against the people. I don't think this is what the liberal university circles from which I come want.... Perhaps there has been a lack of political clear-sightedness and determination, but there certainly is goodwill there.

"Our political-military organizations, especially the Farabundo Martí FPL, are interested in receiving contributions from all sectors, because otherwise, we cannot wage the struggle to benefit the people.

"I'd like to say to the university professors, to my teachers, the liberal sector, and to the small and middle proprietors, farmers, business people, that the popular revolution is not directed against them....Bourgeois propaganda tries to sell them that idea to get them on their side. Our revolution is against the capitalist oligarchical power, it is against the repressive apparatus that defends that power and it is against imperialist intervention that also feeds and defends that power....It is not against the middle sectors, nor against the low productivity economic units....On the contrary we want to rally the greatest possible number of social sectors....The broader, more determined and solid the incorporation into the struggle, the less costly it will be and more quickly it will be carried out, to the good of the people."

OPTIMISM AND CONCERN

█ How do you see El Salvador's future?

"I regard it with optimism and with healthy revolutionary concern. With optimism, because on observing the last few years of our political process, it is clear there is a high degree of maturity and willingness on the part of our popular organizations....I also look upon it with concern because I think that the final phase to destroy the apparatus of domination is going to be very difficult.

"Above all, I have complete confidence in the people's victory, but even after the political-military victory, the efforts to build a society in the direction of socialism, the efforts to put people's power in practice are going to be very difficult and will come up against many obstacles....This is a country with few resources, and I think we're going to have difficulties....It has five million inhabitants....I feel that the difficulties, to mention a nearby example, will be far greater than those faced or to be faced by the Nicaraguan process.

"In this regard I feel that genuine revolutionaries must always keep in mind that their goal is the construction of a just society, free of exploitation, a society in which there will truly be equality and liberty and economic, cultural and all manner of development....

"To those who suffered disillusionment over the failure of the previous government, I'd say, on the contrary, that they should be motivated to deepen the struggle with optimism and realize that now, more than ever before, we must fight with determination and have faith in the people....I have faith in the Salvadorean people, because there is no power in the world, no matter how great, that can defeat an entire people determined to win their freedom."

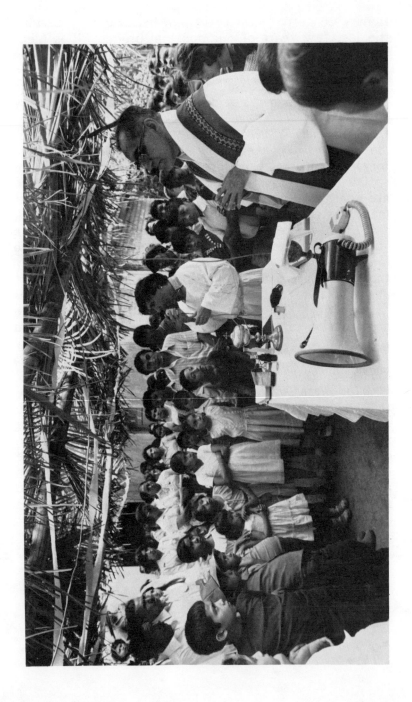

III
With
Monseñor
Romero

ARCHBISHOP OSCAR ROMERO

With Monseñor Romero

"Christians are not afraid to fight. They are capable of fighting but prefer to speak the language of peace. However, when a dictatorship seriously attacks human rights and the commonweal of the nation, when it becomes unbearable and all channels of dialogue, understanding and rationality are closed off; when this happens, then the Church speaks of the legitimate right to insurrectional violence," Dr. Oscar Arnulfo Romero, archbishop of San Salvador for the past two years, told Prensa Latina in an exclusive interview.

Deeply concerned over the spiral of uncontainable violence, the spiritual guide of the Salvadorean Catholics stressed that the "common enemy of our people is the oligarchy - read, the fourteen families - an increasingly insatiable oligarchy to whom I shout this warning: open your hands, give your rings, because the time will come when you will have your hands cut off!"

A man of the people, simple and modest, Monsignor Romero unreservedly defends the interests of the dispossessed, whom he urges to better their organization "to fight effectively for an authentic society with social justice and freedom."

His words are like a relentless whip that scourges not only those who monopolize wealth and fight structural changes, but also the military elite that has transformed the vast fortunes of the fourteen families into a national security issue and institutionalized the insecurity of the majority of the people.

The 62-year-old Romero has turned Sunday mass in the Cathedral of San Salvador into a center of political attention for worshipers, the national and overseas press and, of course, for those who never attend but always hear about his messages: those who are responsible for the violence.

Thus, the killings, disappearances, arbitrary arrests, torture, acts of terrorism, that is, all that goes against human dignity, is denounced each week by this Cato of a church which is aware that change will come with or without it, but which, by its very nature, must stand committed to the Salvadorean people's efforts to attain social liberation.

This "voice of the voiceless" rings out clear and precise: it accuses the criminals by their full names. And recently, from the pulpit of the Cathedral, Monsignor Romero demanded the resignation of none other than Colonel José Guillermo García, the key man in the first, and in the current, ruling junta, its minister of defense and public security.

His "upright evangelism" has meant that the archbishop of San Salvador has not escaped attack from the far right, although so far he has managed to escape death.* He has been the victim of several attacks on his life, which he refers to as "crowns of thorns, at times very hard," but about which he would rather not speak because "the Church is dutybound to stand in solidarity with the poor, in their risks and their persecution. The Church must be prepared to provide the supreme testimony of love to defend and promote those whom Jesus loved above all others."

A priest for 38 years now, Monsignor Oscar Arnulfo Romero recently received two European prizes, elo-

---

* Archbishop Romero was assassinated on March 24, 1980 by one of the Salvadorean government's death squads led by Roberto D'Aubuisson, currently the President of El Salvador's Constituent Assembly.

quent testimony to international solidarity with his work as "pillar of truth" in a country where a corrupt press has forced the people to express themselves on rocks in the fields and on the walls of buildings. In addition, the objective behind the occupation of churches and embassies - and some kidnappings - is none other than to draw world attention to the Salvadorean drama.

THE CAUSE OF THE VIOLENCE IS THE OLIGARCHY

In his home in the Oncological Hospital of the Divine Providence, far from his native Barrios, a town in the department of San Miguel in the eastern part of the country, the archbishop made an exception and granted us an exclusive interview:

What do you regard as the cause of violence in El Salvador?

"The cause of all our ills is the oligarchy, that handful of families who care nothing for the hunger of the people but need that hunger to be able to have available cheap, abundant labor to raise and export their crops....National and foreign-owned industrial companies' competitiveness on the international market comes from starvation wages, and this explains their all-out opposition to any kind of reform or union organizing designed to improve the living standards of the popular sectors....The oligarchy does not allow labor or peasant organizing, because it sees it as inimical to its economic interests. And repression against the people becomes, for that handful of families, a necessity for maintaining and increasing their profit levels, at the cost of the growing poverty of the working people....

"Now, the absolutization of wealth and property brings absolutization of political, economic and social power, without which it is impossible to maintain privileges, even at the cost of human dignity itself. In our country, that is the root of structural violence and oppressive violence and, in the last analysis, is the prime cause of our economic, political and social underdevelopment....The armed forces are in charge of protecting the interests of the oligarchy, of guarding the economic and political structure with the pretext that it is the national interest and security. All those who are not in agreement with the state are declared enemies of the nation, and the most execrable acts are justified as necessary for national security....Everything here is geared to the interests of the oligarchy, an all-powerful oligarchy that feels utter scorn for the people and their rights....In this way, the interests and benefit of a handful are absolutized. This absolutization is mystified, as if the national security system - which seeks to cloak itself in a subjective profession of Christian faith - were the only or the best "defender of Christian civilization," and the "democratic ideals of the West."

"The noble role of the armed forces is twisted out of shape: instead of serving the genuine national interest, they become the guardians of the interests of the oligarchy, thus fomenting their own economic and ideological corruption. And the same can be said of the security bodies: instead of watching out for civic order, they are repressive bodies used against those who oppose the oligarchy...."

ABOUT THE POPULAR ORGANIZATIONS

What is your opinion, Monsignor, of the Popular Revolutionary Bloc, the 28th of February Popular Leagues, FAPU, the National Democratic Union and other mass organizations, which, to be sure, speak of you with tremendous respect and greatly esteem your work at the head of the Church?

"....I am happy that all those organizations which are sincerely seeking the transformation of society, which are seeking a just order, recognize the sincerity with which I try to serve my dioceses....Precisely when the repression against those organizations has been at its worst, I have taken up, and continue to take up, their defense....In my third pastoral letter I defended the right to organize, and, in the name of the Gospel, I pledged to support all that is just in their demands and denounce all attempts to destroy them.

"Now, in the country's present situation, I believe

more than ever in the mass organizations; I believe in the real need of the Salvadorean people to organize, because I believe that the mass organizations are the social forces that will push, that will pressure for an authentic society, with social justice and liberty.... Organization is necessary to struggle effectively....But I have also been frank with the mass organizations, and that is a service which the Church offers, that is, to point out possible errors and injustices. And I do so, I repeat, because those organizations are necessary for the process of liberation and cannot and must not lose sight of their reason for being: they are a social force for the good of the people....Fanaticism and sectarianism, which prevent building up a dialogue and alliances, must be avoided....In politics, my role is that of shepherd: to orient, guide, point to more efficient objectives....And because I esteem the mass organizations, I feel a great satisfaction with the spirit of unity, which is coming about in actual practice....The commonweal must be saved by all of us together...."

ABOUT THE PERSECUTION OF THE CHURCH

Monsignor, El Salvador is a country where the immense majority of the population profess the Catholic religion. However, priests who promote full human liberation are kidnapped, tortured and murdered. Among others, there are the cases of Fathers Grande, Barrero Moto, Navarro Oviedo, Octavio Ortíz. What is your opinion?

"Yes, the contrast is a very big one....I have often reflected on this, and I've reached the conclusion that the situation of social injustice is so grave it has reached a point at which faith itself has been perverted, transformed into a crime to defend economic, material interests....Now, if a state of perversion has been reached, you yourself have underlined the fact that the victims have been precisely those most committed to the liberation of the Salvadorean people. Then, an explanation arises: those priests called for change, they prompted it, and they organized workers and peasants, but the oligarchy opposes all changes, all organization; it does not want to hear the words agrarian reform, or anything else that would mean even the slightest modification in the present situation. Its wealth, its holdings, its ideas, are, and represent, the nation; hence the whole thing links up with the 'security' of El Salvador, and anything that endangers the security of the country must be eliminated....The priests you mentioned 'attacked the social structure,' and by so doing became 'subversives,' 'Communists,' and as such they were persecuted and murdered....Those exemplary priests, worthy of all respect and admiration, were victims of the desire to preserve an unjust order....Because Barrero Moto, Rutilio Grande, Navarro Oviedo, Ortíz and others were farsighted, they perceived reality with total clarity and declared that the common enemy of our people is the oligarchy. Because of this, they were hated and persecuted to death by the oligarchy and the guardians of its wealth...."

In your opinion, what should the role of the Church be in the liberation process of the Salvadorean people?

"Above all, that it be the Church; that is, identity and authenticity, to confront an environment of lies and lack of sincerity, where truth itself is enslaved to the interests of wealth and power....Injustice must be called by its right name, and the truth must be served.... Exploitation of man by man must be denounced as also discrimination, violence inflicted upon human beings, against the interests of the people, their spirit, their conscience and their convictions.... Full liberation of man must be promoted....The Church must call for structural changes, accompany the people in their fight for liberation....An authentic church is dutybound to stand alongside the poor, in solidarity with their risks and their destiny of persecution; the Church must stand ready to bear supreme witness of its love to defend those whom Jesus loved above all others...."

On more than a few occasions you have stressed the work of the Christian communities in El

Salvador. However, several of their leaders, such as Apolinario Serrano and Felipe de Jesús Chacón - father of the secretary general of the Popular Revolutionary Bloc -have been brutally murdered, their faces skinned, their eyes gouged and tongues cut out. A similar fate has been met by catechists and people taking Christianity courses. They were all men of peace who acted in keeping with the orientations of the Church. And so I wonder what course is open to a people who are killed for using peaceful means in their quest for social justice?

"I am grateful to you for mentioning those names, because to me, especially, they are very dear: Felipe de Jesús Chacón, Polín - as we called Apolinario. I have truly wept for them, and for many others who were catechists, workers in our communities, very Christian men. One man who was murdered in Aguilares was known as 'the man of the Gospel....' A deeply felt religion leads to political commitments and must give rise to conflicts in a country like ours, in which social injustice holds sway.

"That was the case of the priests we were talking about....They were essentially good human beings, and they were deeply loved by the people; they laid bare social injustice, they exalted human dignity, the dignity of peasants and workers, of those dispossessed by the oligarchy....Men who organized the people, who helped do so, because this is fundamental to effective struggle....This is an invaluable service, and that is why they were murdered by the oligarchy in alliance with the soldiers, the police, the national guards, paramilitary bands....Those killings accentuate the degree of perversion that has been reached by the worshippers of insatiable Moloch....Now, and this is stressed in Populorum Progressio, Christians are not afraid to fight; they are capable of fighting, but they prefer to speak the language of peace. However, when a dictatorship seriously attacks human rights and the commonweal of the nation, when it becomes unbearable, and all channels of dialogue, understanding and rationality are closed off, when this happens, then the Church speaks of the legitimate right to insurrectional violence.... Choosing the moment of insurrection, determining when all channels of dialogue are closed off, is not up to the Church....I shout this warning to the oligarchy: open your hands, give your rings, because the time will come when you will have your hands cut off!"

Christmas Eve and New Year's Eve were tragic in El Salvador: hundreds of people were murdered by the repressive bodies. It was as if sadistic minds had chosen those dates to plunge more Salvadorean homes into mourning. The newspapers and the radio, with a few exceptions that confirm the rule, lied about the events, distorted the truth. They also evidenced a degree of corruption that would be hard to surpass. Monsignor Romero, what do you feel the role of the press should be?

"Yes, the corruption of the press is part of our sad situation; it reveals complicity with the oligarchy....The role of the press must be that of channeling information on the truth....Unfortunately here, as you have pointed out, the situation is the exact opposite: the news is manipulated, serious incidents implicating the oligarchy are silenced, news items on repression are distorted, victims are made out to be guilty; photographs are falsified, composite photos are mounted to deceive readers....What more can I say? The truth is withheld, the truth is not spoken in El Salvador....I have denounced this situation many times....I have stressed that the press should be an instrument at the service of the people for the transformation of society....A great deal of power is lost in this way, and placed at the service of oppression and repression!"

Recently Salvador Samayoa, minister of education during the two months that the first ruling junta held office, disclosed the real reasons for his resignation. He warned that El Salvador's problems cannot be solved through peaceful means and announced that he was joining the ranks of the

Farabundo Martí Popular Liberation Forces. What is your opinion of Samayoa's decision?

"In such cases, above all, I respect the option the person takes, especially when the person involved is intelligent, like Samayoa, who I feel certain has acted according to his conscience. A conscience, moreover, is worthy of respect, and God will judge each of us according to our own conscience....Now, as a shepherd of the Church, I cannot advise anyone to choose the course of violence....However the lesson that Samayoa has afforded us consists of denouncing, once again, that those who are really responsible for violence in our country are the families making up the oligarchy; that those who close off peaceful ways for solving problems are the idolaters of wealth....Samayoa's decision amounts to a grave denunciation, it is an 'I accuse' that is thoroughly timely and which should invite people to reflect...."

Monsignor Romero, as archbishop of San Salvador, do you not have the opportunity of speaking with the military high commands?

"Yes, I do, and my language is always the same: I speak the truth and I guide within the framework of my pastoral role....I am in favor of all that can serve the people, and if it is claimed that there is a conflict between the government and my archdiocese, the formulation is a mistaken one. What there is, is a conflict between the government and the people, and my Church is always with the people....The oligarchy and the military elite do not want dialogue, are not prepared to accept dialogue...."

What do you see as the outlook for the present military and Christian Democratic government?

"Before giving an opinion, I would prefer to wait and see what happens....Changes are urgently needed, because the people are no longer waiting; they are frustrated, disillusioned and no longer believe in promises or in hopes....I would say, then, that the changes must be spectacular ones...."

 During my travels around the country, I've had the impression that there's civil war in El Salvador, and that it is becoming less and less irregular and intermittent and more and more relentless. What is your view?

"The situation I find alarming. But the oligarchy's fight to defend the indefensible has no future, less so taking into consideration our people's fighting spirit. The forces of the oligarchy might even come up with fleeting victory, but the voice of justice of our people would make itself heard again, and, sooner rather than later, they will win out. The new society is coming, and it's coming fast....The peace of the cemeteries, because in the graves there are only the dead. And that kind of peace cannot be obtained by the oligarchy against a people like the Salvadorean people...."

And in that war, Monsignor Romero, you, as shepherd, will continue by your people's side?

"That is my aim, and I ask God to help me to be strong enough, because I fear the weakness of the flesh....In difficult times, we are all afraid; the instinct of self-preservation is very strong, and that is why I ask for help....help not only for myself, but for all those who are engaged in this pastoral work, help to remain at our posts, because we have a great deal to do, be it only to gather in the dead and absolve the dying....The flame of social justice must always remain alive in the heart of the Salvadorean people...."

IV

With the Party of the Salvadorean Revolution/

Revolutionary Army of the People (PRS/ERP)

JOAQUIN VILLALOBOS

A perspective of power opens

The school is somewhat out of the ordinary, but it is certainly the most effective: the school of errors, in which teachers and students, protagonists of the most painful, heartrending mistakes, reflect on the basis of the confusion and bewilderment that their political behavior has occasioned among a people involved in a revolutionary process; a singular school in which not only are the mistakes recognized in direct contact with the population but are corrected in the midst of popular struggle, until a course is found that will make it possible to move forward with certainty and determination.

A school of this kind exists in this country at war, with unquestionable sway and a familiar name, the People's Revolutionary Army (ERP), whose most advanced members, linked with large influential sectors of the dispossed majority that wants unity of action among the revolutionary and democratic organizations, have built a Party of the Salvadorean Revolution (PRS), a solid organization for the masses with political and military force.

The synthesis of this concrete experience also has a name, Joaquín Villalobos, "René Cruz" in the underground, general secretary of the PRS and also the top leader of the ERP.

For several hours Prensa Latina interviewed this 28-year-old leader who left his studies in economics to become a full-time revolutionary. The interview was conducted in the home of a typical Salvadorean working class family, a suitable setting for reflecting the sincerity, simplicity, flexibility, and spirit of unity that today characterize the members of the PRS-ERP.

REGARDING MILITARISM AND ITS CONSEQUENCES

However, before presenting the main portions of the interview with Joaquín Villalobos, it should be pointed out that the complex process of development begun by the ERP in 1971 and that emerged from sharp contradictions, reached a qualitatively higher stage at the 1st Congress of the Party of the Salvadorean Revolution, held in 1977.

The Congress witnessed the end of pragmatism, nearsightedness, the thirst for power and individual control, and militarism, with their wake of tragic consequences, which for several years determined the course of the People's Revolutionary Army and hindered the initial stage of existence of the PRS.

The line regarding short-term victory generated military conceptions and solutions for every type of activity or problem and reflected a profound underestimation, even scorn, for the revolutionary movement of the Salvadorean masses, channeled through different methods, forms and means of struggle.

Militarism for its part not only isolated the ERP from the people but from the very development of the political process in El Salvador. Because it expected a rapid denouement of class contradictions and spent its time preparing the instruments of war, the ERP was unable to influence the forces that were developing in the critical phases of the social movement.

In addition, the hegemonic ambitions manifested by its top leader at the time, Sebastián Urquilla, prevented internal discussion and democracy, encouraged sectarianism and factionalism in the ERP ("divide and conquer") and made way for adventurism, whose clearest expression was Carlos Humberto Portillo (Mario Vladimir Rogel) and the summary executions to settle political contradictions. Due to this, prestigious members of the ERP were slain, including poet Roque Dalton García.

As a logical consequence of the foregoing, the ERP underwent even greater division, with the most important faction comprised of the sectors that today have become an influential political-military organization, the National Resistance (RN).

REQUIREMENTS OF THE PROCESS

Returning to a principled policy was anything but easy. However, revolution is a complex whole, and the objective reality of the Salvadorean revolutionary process called for urgent changes.

Thus, when the instrument of criticism and self-criticism began to be used by the most advanced members - precisely by those who displayed their heroism in military operations on the basis of which they came to realize the need for a link with the mass movement and unity with the other revolutionary and democratic organizations - the door was open for collective discussion, and the organization's military structure and verticalism began to crumble.

In the process of rectification, a special place is held by Rafael Antonio Arce Zablah, "Amílcar," killed on September 26, 1975, during the withdrawal following the military occupation of the village of Carmen, in the eastern department of La Union.

ENCOUNTER WITH THE PRESENT

"The road has been very difficult and bitter. Recovery has meant big sacrifices, but the results are there to be seen today," says Octavio Ponce, member of the Political Commission of the PRS and of the General Staff of the ERP, while he took me to the place where I was to meet Joaquín Villalobos.

"We have matured and improved our discipline in the course of the past few years. Today we are sure that we possess the mechanisms which, without undermining the dynamics of ideological struggle - the motor that moves us in the direction of correct positions - guarantee the unity of the Party," declared the leader who nine years ago was one of the founding members of the ERP.

■ What do you mean by unity?

Octavio replied, "We mean the confidence of all the Party cadres and rank and file members in democratic centralism, which corrects any possible deviation...."

The PRS-ERP security measures are similar to those used by the Farabundo Martí Popular Liberation Forces and the other Salvadorean political-military organizations. They reply upon the population, among whom the Party members move like fish in water.

Joaquín Villalobos chose the home of a working class family to spend the night.

"If we fight and work with them, naturally we live with them too," said Villalobos as he introduced the writer to his hosts, who welcomed us warmly, pleased that the truth about their struggle would be published. We all got ready for the interview, and the combatants settled down to listen to their top leader.

PART OF THE SALVADOREAN POLITICAL VANGUARD

■ What are the PRS and the ERP?

"In regard to the Party, we could answer with a definition: it is the detachment of political cadres that enable us to tackle the task of leading the struggle of the masses to get their demands met, as well as the political-military struggle. Inside the organization, it helps us to establish the forms and methods that promote the political, tactical, and strategic capacity of the cadres, who are guided by democratic centralism.

"As for the ERP, maybe we could say that it was the seed that generated the Party and which today is the seed of the People's Army. However, the main thing is that we look upon both the Party and the Army as a part of the most advanced political detachment, that is, as a part of the vanguard of the Salvadorean revolution."

█ Why were they created?

"To answer that, we should briefly say something about the history of the PRS and the ERP, two different instruments of struggle but with many points in common. The ERP came into being in 1971 as part of an upsurge of revolutionary activity and concern manifested within the political organizations then existing in the country....Basically, the ERP came into being in answer to the need to create and organize the armed apparatuses that would make it possible to carry out new forms of struggle in the Salvadorean revolutionary process....This was an initial solution, which implied little clearsightedness at the time....The organization was chaotic, comprised as it was of different groups with different approaches to strategy but sharing the desire to promote armed struggle in El Salvador.

"Subsequently, all that began to be channeled towards a process in which the guerrilla cadres reflect, mature, process their experience and start to acquire a political vision requiring links with the masses and a structure that permits suitable political work....Thus, greater application of experiences led us on the course of building a Party....Amidst that hazardous process, fraught with difficulties - internal divisions, splits, - a Party began to take shape, with serious discussion. That was in 1975. The process culminated two years later, in 1977, with the 1st Congress. The main strategic changes came about, among them the eradication of militarism from the organization.

"As for the Army, it is now under the political leadership and its structure has been modified. We realized, despite the fact that the influence of verticalism was still present, that the process of the Salvadorean revolution and its leadership were fundamentally political. So, the main thing was to establish the mechanisms for an adequate channeling of political and military problems....Because they are historic necessities, the Party and the Army exist...."

THE INSURRECTIONAL LINE: TODAY'S THESIS

[?] What is the strategy of the PRS-ERP?

"Our strategy is that of the people's revolutionary war. Imperialism is the fundamental strategic enemy in alliance with the national oligarchy and the most reactionary sectors of the army. In this framework, we look upon the process of founding the ERP as part of the building and shaping of the strategic revolutionary forces that will make possible the defeat of the enemies of the Salvadorean people....

"However, despite the fact that the PRS-ERP has as its strategy the people's revolutionary war, we must not lose sight of the fact that we arrived on the Salvadorean scene during a profound economic and political crisis in Central America, which meant that the revolutionary forces that emerged during the period would have to assume basic historic commitments in the framework of a real policy on power in view of the weakening of imperialism, the oligarchy and the lackey governments in the area.

"In this regard, in the stage that triggered off the revolutionary war of the people, the PRS-ERP presented as its fundamental thesis the implementation of an insurrectional line, which was first put forward in 1975, perhaps without all the necessary theoretical and political considerations, but essentially it was correct. The critical process generated within the governments at the service of the oligarchy and the wearing away that they have undergone at the hands of the revolutionary organizations, as well as the deterioration of imperialism internationally, have created the conditions to proceed from guerrilla warfare and building an army with a strategic view, to a fundamental phase of the struggle for power: the phase of the accelerated development of insurrection, which we see in the short or medium term."

THE BASIC PROBLEMS

[?] What are the immediate and medium-term objectives of the PRS-ERP?

"What other revolutionary movements might regard as long-range objectives become in the Salvadorean revolutionary process short- and medium-term goals. With regard to the former, we regard as vitally important the solution of problems connected with the unity of all the left-wing forces....Given the fact that at this time a power prospect is opening up not only for the Salvadorean revolution but for the Central American revolution, and given the fact, in addition, that this prospect exists for the anti-imperialist forces in Latin America as a whole, in the concrete reality of the Salvadorean situation failure to achieve the left-wing unity that would mean a new victory for the Latin American revolution would amount to a betrayal of the interests of that revolution, in our opinion.

"As for the medium-term objectives, we believe they are the same for all the forces that make up the vanguard of the Salvadorean revolution: the taking of power and the establishment of a popular democratic government leading towards socialism, or a government that would be defined by all the revolutionary forces in alliance with the most advanced democratic sectors."

What is the place of the PRS-ERP in the Salvadorean people's struggle?

"The crisis in Salvadorean society cannot be seen in isolation from the Central American crisis, of whose economic structure El Salvador is a part. The essential economic and political problems are so interrelated that the existence or the change of one of those phenomena in one of the countries of the region conditions the existence and the change of other phenomena in several or all the other countries of Central America. The region must be seen as a dialectical unity of opposites, with the Central American countries standing as the opposites....

"The crisis exists as a whole, in Central America, and also as a specific factor, that is, in each nation.... This crisis, therefore, has a two-fold nature, so to speak. At certain intervals, social explosions are to be expected in the process of the sharpening of the Central American economic and political crisis: Nicaragua, El Salvador, Guatemala....In addition, the same identity of phenomena also occurs between the peoples and their revolutionary vanguards, which conceive of the revolution in its two-fold nature, specific, Salvadorean, and general, Central American.

"Moreover, the present crisis of the economic and political structures of Central America is manifested at a time in which imperialism, in our opinion, is fighting a defensive battle....

"This sets guidelines for the Central American process to become a series of victories for the Latin American revolution, to become a liberation process, not only from the geographical standpoint, but also from the political standpoint of the other revolutionary vanguard of Latin America...."

POLITICAL OFFENSIVE OF THE PEOPLE

What are the objectives of occupying cities, villages, hamlets, estates and factories?

"Although each political-military organization regards occupying places in terms of its tactical objectives, the main thing is to analyze the meaning of such occupations for the Salvadorean revolutionary process. The occupations are part of an offensive by the masses, a policy which no longer accepts the rules of the game established by the oligarchy and the military regimes, nor the formulas of imperialism, such as the present ruling junta.

"The occupations are part of the struggle by the masses for wage improvements, for increased fringe benefits or for political objectives, such as to denounce cases of persons who have disappeared, killings, torture practices, and to demand the release of political prisoners. In their most advanced stage, military occupation by the revolutionary organizations generates the conditions for a growing process of insurrectional struggle...."

However, the violence has increased. Scores of people are killed for peacefully occupying estates owned by the fourteen families. Why does the PRS-ERP insist on using those methods?

"The tactical objectives of an occupation could be formulated as winning concrete points, but the important thing is that they express a political situation, a degree of tension that is accentuated day by day....The final outcome is sought with methods, forms and means of going on the offensive; if the occupations were stopped, it could mean that the masses fall back on the defensive....This doesn't mean that we should pursue a wait-and-see policy and respond blow by blow; better tactics need to be adopted to prevent repressive operations by the regime."

What does the PRS-ERP think of the Church?

"In our country, among the forces acting at the center of this society in conflict, the Church has played one of the most important and courageous roles. The revolutionary organizations are not unaware of the role played by the democratic sectors that seek a revolutionary solution to the crisis of Salvadorean society. Within those broad social forces, the Catholic Church plays a key role.

"And in this regard it should be pointed out that the grass-roots level of the Salvadorean Church is closely linked with the popular sectors. This is to be explained by the religious work done by the Church in the communities, neighborhoods, villages and slum areas. The Church in El Salvador is endowed with extraordinary social sensitivity and is politically very close to the revolutionary and democratic forces."

Urgent necessity:
the coordination of the struggle

"The unity of the revolutionary and democratic organizations is a vital necessity at this historic moment, when a prospect for power is opening up and the Salvadorean oligarchy and its reactionary forces, in alliance with imperialism, are going on the defensive....This could well be the year of unity, the year that marks the start of the great, decisive battles for the definitive liberation of El Salvador," declared Joaquín Villalobos, general secretary of the Party of the Salvadorean Revolution (PRS) and top leader of the People's Revolutionary Army (ERP) in an exclusive interview with Prensa Latina.

"This historic moment," added the young strategist of a policy for people's power and organization for promoting the development of the insurrectional process, "is a phase in which imperialism is going on the strategic defensive in Central America, a zone that is vital for its interests in Latin America....

"This is also the phase of the overall defense of the capitalist system under Central American oligarchic rule....which explains the unity of the oligarchies and their military instruments for the defense of their wealth...."

AUDACITY AS A POLITICAL THESIS

 What is the PRS-ERP's view on audacity?

"In this regard, we must refer to our experiences. Evidently, audacity is conceived of as a political thesis for being able to act in any revolutionary process. Had it not been for rapid decisions, had we not acted at given times because the military disadvantage weighed more, had we not taken into account the great political, ideological and moral advantage existing in the masses, we would certainly not have succeeded in growing and we would have fallen into vacillations....

"Precisely for that reason, we regard audacity as essential for the revolutionary process, and this has not been limited to the PRS-ERP but is a constant of the other Salvadorean revolutionary organizations. Perhaps one of the most audacious steps we have taken so far was the insurrection of October 16, 1979, the day after the General Carlos Humberto Romero government toppled. For 12 hours, and in some cases for longer, we militarily occupied several villages, where lengthy combats took place, and in that fighting we were supported by the local people. The material means were few, but the morale of the masses was outstanding. Popular political and ideological readiness for combat is simply beyond discussion. Now, why did we decide to conduct those actions? Because the overthrow of Romero was an imperialist maneuver, and this has been fully demonstrated, to deceive the Salvadorean people. Had it become consolidated, it would have meant a defeat, of a temporary nature to be sure, but all the same a defeat for a revolutionary alternative.

"At that time, any defense of the revolutionary alternative had to be audacious and determined. In fact, it was necessary to run all the risks involved, beginning with the loss of our cadres....The objective was strategic: to save the revolutionary process...."

OBJECTIVES OF THE PRESENT RULING JUNTA

 What does the PRS-ERP think of the present ruling junta?

"Before expressing our opinion on the present alliance between the military and the Christian Democratic Party, we should outline the problems arising during the two and a half months of the first (post-Romero) junta. On the one hand, how do you explain the internal situation of that government and its contradictory social makeup? On the other, how do you define the political picture to the masses in order to adjust our line of action? If we had spoken out on the inner contradictions in the junta, we would have confused the masses.

"We couldn't adopt a stance on the basis of the intentions of the civilian personalities, who lacked decision-making power and were unable to apply reforms and changes in practice. Rather, we had to assess matters on the basis of the prime element in the ruling junta, the armed forces, which held power and were not about to agree to any deep-going, radical changes, because their objectives were counterrevolutionary, to isolate the people from their vanguard and attempt to destroy the revolutionary political-military organizations....

"And so, regardless of the good intentions of the personalities belonging to that first ruling junta, our policy consisted of applying constant pressure so that the military sectors that were really running the government would be forced to take up the defense of the true scheme of imperialism, the oligarchy and their allies....

"Militant pressure by the masses and revolutionary actions of a military nature speeded up the crisis of the first ruling junta.

"The democratic officials resigned, and the maneuvers of the enemies of the people were exposed. Now, the alliance between the military and the Christian Democrats faces many political disadvantages, including a low level of credibility and very few possibilities for resolving problems....

"Moreover, it is important to stress the following: the present ruling junta knows where it wants to go and how to act, that is, there is unity regarding objectives and methods. That is the essential difference between the present government and the first ruling junta, within which the democrats who demanded changes and the end of the repression clashed with those who were determined not to let any of that happen.

"Hence the military and the Christian Democratic personalities who make up the present government are perfectly aware of the rules of the game: promise lots of reforms, make a minimum of concessions and go all out in repressing the people. The reactionary current in the Christian Democratic Party headed by José Napoleón Duarte is aware that repression is needed, and the military are aware that this current is in agreement with the repression in order to stop the revolutionary offensive of the masses."

REAL AND PERMANENT COORDINATION

What is the opinion of the PRS-ERP regarding the unity of the revolutionary and democratic forces in El Salvador?

"Right now, that may well be one of the key points of the Salvadorean revolutionary process. To give you a broad reply, we could raise the following questions: Why is unity needed? How do we think unity should be brought about at this time? How should the unity process be combined with a broad policy of alliances?

"In regard to the first question, that is, on the need for unity, we feel that the economic, political and social crisis of Salvadorean society is a solid, basic argument.

"The unity of the revolutionary and democratic organizations is a vital necessity of this historic moment, when a prospect for power is opening up and the Salvadorean oligarchy and its reactionary forces, in alliance with imperialism, are going on the defensive.

"And it is a phase in which imperialism is going on the strategic defensive in Central America, a vital zone when it comes to its interests in the continent. This is also the phase of the overall defense of the capitalist system under Central American oligarchal rule.... which explains the unity of the oligarchies and their

101

military instruments for the defense of their wealth.

"In the context, failure to regard unity as a formidable political-military instrument that would enable the revolutionary and democratic organizations, acting as a whole, to take advantage of the maximum potential of their forces at a time in which a power prospect is opening up, would mean failure to fulfill a basic task of the Salvadorean and also of the Latin American revolution.

"At this point, the idea isn't to wage a debate on political lines, since when it comes to concrete reality, we are all acting in unison for the same goals and we are all under attack by the forces led by imperialism, and they make no distinction between one revolutionary political-military organization and another....

"Now, just how do we think that unity should be achieved? We feel it should be achieved in ways that will give it strategic scope. In this regard, we are not party to the traditional concept of unity, that is, of organic unity established overnight, which tries to overlook the different styles, concepts, language, etc. that characterize each revolutionary organization.

"We look upon unity as a process built up from a permanent coordination, not circumstantial or under the control of the revolutionary forces. And by coordination we mean genuine, frank coordination, which has the Salvadorean revolution as its main goal. That would be followed by organic stages in building the most advanced political detachment for leading the Salvadorean revolution, on the basis of the revolutionary forces as a whole.

"That is our view on how unity conceived of as a process, should be brought about, without setting any time limits. However, we do feel that, because of the requirements of the Salvadorean revolution, the process to which we refer ought not to take a year; it could take just a few months. And we say this because contacts in the grassroots level between the different revolutionary organizations and contacts in implementing our lines indicate that if coordination is established, the organizations will be brought together fast.

"What are the problems we confront in the process

leading to unity? At first there were problems regarding essential differences in political lines, especially during the period of the first ruling junta.

"But there are other problems whose solution will mean that the coordination process must establish ways and means for eliminating subjectivism, reservations arising from the way the ideological struggle was conducted in the past. Today there aren't any political differences among the revolutionary organizations, but subjectivism almost forces them into being because different organizations are involved.

"We need to fight subjectivism. And unity must be viewed as political unity in which all the forces of the Salvadorean revolution will take part, even those which so far have not played an important role, but which - and this is very important - must not be cut off from the revolutionary forces as a whole.

"And then, how do we view unity from the standpoint of alliances with the democratic forces? We feel that we need to take a broad view regarding the participation of the democratic forces as part of a policy enabling the revolutionary forces to show them how the revolutionary forces are forces of change that stand for genuine people's democracy....Correct application of such a policy would deprive imperialism, and the sectors of the oligarchy that serve as its strategic tools, of allies for a possible bid to implant new policies of domination....

"In this regard we feel our criterion has to be a broad one, enabling the revolutionary forces to win over the democratic forces. And to that end, we need to reach an understanding, adopt broad platforms and wording. The revolutionary forces cannot and must not forget the need for a joint policy regarding the democratic forces, so that policy can fulfill the two-fold function of encouraging the popular masses and inspiring confidence in the revolutionary left as an alternative for the democratic forces."

 Attacks have been made on the lives of several figures who resigned from the first ruling junta. What does the PRS-ERP have to say about this?

"When these attacks took place, we immediately issued statements condemning them, to show the honest, consistently democratic forces that we revolutionaries have a clear view of the principal enemy and that we certainly do not regard as enemies people who honestly and honorably attempted to apply a process of changes as members of the first ruling junta....

"Moreover, if the revolutionary forces applied a policy of responding to repressive actions or murders by the reactionary right-wing, that does not mean that criminal attacks on persons belonging to the democratic forces will go unpunished. Those attacks have the political objective of weakening the possibilities of the convergence of the democratic and the revolutionary sectors."

A WEAPON FOR PUNISHING THE OLIGARCHY

▌▌ What is the opinion of the PRS-ERP on kidnapping?

"We look upon kidnapping operations as acts of revolutionary justice. In this society, one of the poorest and sickest, it is hard to describe the repression. Truly savage, vicious acts are committed against a population who lack the most vital necessities. For instance, an operation in which the revolutionary forces seize, for the purposes of justice, one member of the families that wield economic and political power on the basis of the exploitation of the people, becomes a political instrument that lays bare the structure of injustice and class polarization in this country.

"However, despite the contradictions and the huge responsibility weighing upon a member of the oligarchy or the sectors in its service, the treatment such an individual receives is one of respect towards his person. Even under the conditions of captivity, they are given every comfort possible, while the government or their relatives comply with the demands and conditions demanded by the revolutionary organizations....

"During the time they are held, our Party's policy, in contrast with a deeply reactionary, arrogant, despotic mentality, in contrast with customs of opulence, consists of simple but humane treatment, to show them, in actual practice, the strategy for change for which we revolutionaries are fighting.

"In this framework, the treatment is vastly different from the treatment of persons kidnapped by the repressive bodies at the service of the oligarchy....

"Yes, kidnapping, because, when there is talk of kidnappings or when the Salvadorean media write about kidnapping, they mean the kidnappings carried out by the revolutionary organizations. Such kidnappings have sensational political effects precisely because of the way they're handled by the media, which are owned by the oligarchy or their accomplices....

"However, when the person kidnapped is a Salvadorean working class leader, the act is not assigned political importance, nor is the treatment such persons receive in the secret jails or the garrisons of the regime's security forces. Kidnappings of labor leaders have become basic political acts because they are part of the people's struggle. The treatment meted out to hundreds of prisoners is a political fact that has raised the consciousness of our people....

"When we capture a member of the oligarchy, we give him a book to read: Las cárceles clandestinas de El Salvador (El Salvador's Secret Jails) by Comrade Ana Guadalupe Martínez. The book reports on the treatment of political prisoners: torture, rape, total isolation, no clothes, no food, nothing to sleep on; subhuman conditions in which only revolutionary spirit motivates people to remain alive.

"Little is known about that treatment, because the mass media doesn't report on it. But kidnapping is a fundamental weapon for punishing the oligarchy: they are made to finance the work of the Salvadorean revolution with money stolen from the people."

What price in blood has the PRS-ERP paid in the past nine years?

"The price in blood for building the organization and placing it in the revolutionary struggle of the masses is high. If we were to add up the militia members, the cadres who have taken part in the self-defense of the masses and in guerrilla actions, the figure is more than one hundred. Out of the total number of casualties, there are some with special meaning: Rafael Antonio Arce Zablah, one of the most painful losses, after whom the front in the central part of the country is named; Juan José Gómez, after whom the eastern front is named; Edgard Salmeron, whose name the western front bears. Each of these comrades expresses different stages of the organization's political development, different ways of contributing and synthesizing the highlights of the period of building the organization.

"Then there are other significant losses such as that of Comrade Denis, who fell in the military occupation of San Marcos on October 17, 1979; Comrade Irma Elena Contreras, head of the people's self-defense militia, who was killed in the October 29, 1979 slaughter in San Salvador; and Rodolfo Munguía, killed recently in La Union, who was one of our most important political cadres in the eastern zone. These are perhaps our greatest losses. There are many more, but the losses we have mentioned synthesize different historic moments of our organization and its beginnings in the revolutionary process."

FAMILY UNITY IN THE REVOLUTION

What about the role of women in the PRS-ERP?

"Since the very inception of our organizations, the participation of women has been highly significant. Thirty percent of our Central Committee are women, and one woman comrade is a member of the PRS Political Commission. In our cells, women's participation as political and military cadres is notable.

"Now, this participation is not the result of a line established by the Party leadership but is the reflection of a complex political process involving the masses of the Salvadorean people. In all kinds of political activities, in the struggles of the people, the presence of women, and not only of women, but of entire families, is very common. The participation of the family unit is a very important experience, especially in the rural areas. In the Salvadorean countryside, women cadres are practically strategic, irreplacable pillars. And no kind of differentiation is established in regard to the work women take on...."

THE UNDERGROUND AND THE ROLE OF THE PEOPLE

Notwithstanding this writer's urging, Joaquín Villalobos preferred not to cover his face when pictures were taken of our interview.

▌▌ What is the PRS-ERP's interpretation of the underground?

"When we came into being as an organization, the enemy was just about knocking on the door....The underground, then, became absolutely vital, down to the last detail, because that was the only way for the detachment of cadres to be able to survive. And when we speak of the detachment of cadres, we do not mean just the PRS-ERP but all the others, that is, all the revolutionary organizations that have contributed in one way or another to the fact that right now guidelines are being adopted for a power policy.

"Today, the concept of the underground is beginning to change, becoming more audacious and political.

"It is no longer only a technical method but is beginning to be something in which the masses are starting to plan a role of wider dimensions, of large-scale offensives....If we were to retain an overly-technical concept of the underground, we could even isolate the masses from their military instruments, that is, from the instruments they use to develop the struggle in the political and military spheres....Here in El Salvador, you see this exemplified in the armed defense of the masses in the popular political fronts....

"Here, the rules of the underground take on other characteristics, because there has been a legitimization of the process of self-defense against a savage enemy that has made such forms of organization and such actions valid.

"So, we feel it is absolutely vital to break with some of the requirements of underground existence in order to promote among the masses of the people the notion that their forms of struggle are also forms that establish policies for power, that they are real and that at times they need to be individualized in names, in people, in structures...."

ON INTERNATIONAL POLICY

What about the PRS-ERP's international policy?

"Speaking about our international position involves speaking of the struggle against U.S. imperialism, which we regard as the main enemy of all the peoples and revolutionary movements. In this regard we hail the big contributions made by the peoples of Indochina, especially the Vietnamese, who won the greatest of all victories, forcing imperialist policy to retreat, placing imperialism in a situation of weakness....Despite geographical distance, notwithstanding the natural differences, having a common enemy who was vanquished and weakened by the people of Vietnam made possible the victory of the Nicaraguan people and the future victories of the Salvadorean and Central American revolution.

"We regard all the revolutionary forces of Latin America, especially in the Central American area, and most especially the Cuban revolution, as fundamental, strategic allies of the Salvadorean revolution.

"In defining ourselves as enemies of U.S. imperialism, we also identify with the Non-Aligned Movement, with the struggle of the Palestinian people and of the liberation movements of the African peoples. In a word, we identify with the cause of all the oppressed and exploited peoples."

What about El Salvador's future?

"This could well be the year of unity, the year that marks the start of the great, decisive battles for definitive liberation...."

SCHAFIK HANDAL

V
With the
Communist Party
(PCS)

The founding of the Revolutionary Coordinator of the Masses (CRM).

Late but in time

The determined incorporation of the Communist Party of El Salvador in the armed struggle comes as a historic decision of immediate, far-reaching importance, based on the conviction that "this is the only way to find a genuine solution to the national crisis that will benefit the working people, and the people in general." It has given a big boost to the revolutionary forces of El Salvador, which are now striking out militarily at the forces of the fourteen families and their allies right in the capital of the Republic.

"Our decision was a bit late, but still in time," says Schafik Jorge **Handal,** general secretary of the CPS, in an exclusive interview with Prensa Latina.

The phrase "in time" used by the outstanding theoretician on fascism in Latin America is, in fact, an accurate assessment. The CP decision was made in a context of revolutionary upsurge and of the privileged minority's inability to rule as before. It was then evident to friend and foe alike that there was no possibility for a reformist solution to the problems of hunger, squalor, exploitation and repression that plague this country.

Now, the presence of the Communist Party in the National Coordinating body set up to lead the people's war, is one of the main reasons for the links between important democratic sectors of the "middle class" and the revolutionary political-military organizations.

In the past eleven years, the Communist Party took part, directly or indirectly, in three presidential elections and in six to elect legislators and mayors. The CP stood alongside democratic forces that regarded the electoral road as a possible means to a solution in El Salvador and hoped to be able to bring about changes through Cabinet reshuffles and constitutional amendments. And recently, in a final effort, the Communist Party was also present in the first ruling junta set up after the overthrow of the genocidal regime of General Carlos Humberto Romero on October 15, 1979.

The Communist Party acted in consonance with its commitments to its allies. Its option to join the armed struggle to wipe out the unjust regime in power in the country was adopted after it had been demonstrated that the power of the recalcitrant oligarchy and the forces entrusted with guaranteeing that power, under the auspices of the Pentagon and the transnational corporations, were simply not going to allow any far-reaching reforms. After all is said and done, the facts show that the fourteen families decided just how far a government can go with its superficial, fragmentary changes.

Hence, the democratic forces who went through all that alongside the Communist Party and learned in the tough school of experience, realized that their loyal ally was right in its decision. Today, many of these groups are themselves active participants in the armed struggle.

CP DECISION DIFFICULT AND COMPLEX

The Communist Party's decision was anything but easy. The Party was not prepared for the qualitative leap to a higher form of struggle, and there was no time for a prior process of adjustment. Over 87 percent of its members joined the Party precisely during the years in which it was engaged in open, legal political struggle.

In the process, people developed habits, ideological conceptions, work methods and life styles that were alien to the tough conditions of a political-military process, with its strict security measures and tight regulations designed to guarantee the workings of the revolutionary underground.

Nonetheless, the CP leadership's capacity for change and rectification, applied in the midst of a revolutionary process, and the determination and clear-sightedness of General Secretary Schafik Jorge Handal, meshed with the solidarity of the other revolutionary political-military organizations. As a result, the CPS quickly adjusted to a course with which the vast major-ity of its members were totally unfamiliar. Naturally, this involved difficulties and obstacles, including losses due to inexperience, the torture and death of valuable cadres such as the noted sociologist Roberto Castel-lanos a few days ago, the loss of safe houses and other blows.

But advances take place despite the stumbling blocks, because in addition to the cooperation provided by the other revolutionary forces, insurgent El Salvador is characterized by a climate of confidence, under-standing and respect, and because the members of the CPS are convinced that unity of action is necessary to speed up the end of the hated regime.

And so, these were the conditions prevailing at the time Prensa Latina interviewed Schafik Jorge Handal, an upright leader who is open to all currents of progres-sive thinking, and who enjoys well-deserved prestige among Salvadorean and foreign intellectuals thanks to his work in the social sciences. Theory and practice join hands in the general secretary of the Communist Party, which on March 28, virtually on the threshhold of popular victory, will celebrate its 50th anniversary.

'THIS IS NO LAST MINUTE ABOUT-FACE'

Could you explain why the CPS has opted for armed struggle as the only course to a real solution to the national crisis?

"Practically from its inception, the CPS put forward revolutionary armed struggle as the most likely way to attain victory. It was founded on March 28, 1930, and before its second anniversary, concretely, in January, 1932, the CPS led a large-scale mass insurrection, a great popular revolution composed mainly of peasants.

"Unlike many other Communist Parties, the CPS did not come into being around a group of intellectuals; rather, it emerged from an extraordinary movement of workers in the city and rural countryside.

"Its first leaders were workers. The CPS is the result of a mass movement, and this accounts for its traditionally outstanding ties with the masses. In fact, this is one of the characteristics of the Salvadorean revolutionary movement.

"The 1932 insurrection failed, and over 30,000 workers were killed, including many hundreds of CPS members. The defeat of that attempt to storm the heavens led to a breakdown in the country. The unions disappeared, the activities of the Party were banned in no uncertain terms. An iron-clad, right-wing military dictatorship took over, and it still misrules our country today.

"The CPS was the only organization that managed to survive, albeit in extremely precarious conditions. Notwithstanding, the Party continued to be linked to the masses, and it tried to organize them in those conditions of all-out repression and intolerance.

"In April, 1944, the CPS took part alongside democratic military personnel and civilians in the overthrow of dictator Maximiliano Hernández Martínez. Members of the CPS and workers led by our Party grabbed guns from garrisons whose doors had been opened by democratic military personnel. After three days of savage fighting, the uprising was defeated, but, at the end of the same month and in early May, a successful general strike put an end to the dictatorship.

"In October, 1944, Colonel Aguirre Salinas brought back the military dictatorship, and in December of that year, thousands of young people, workers and students, returned to El Salvador from Guatemala, itself liberated in October, 1944 from the dictatorship of Jorge

Ubico, to take up arms against the usurpers. That revolutionary invasion included Communists and young, anti-imperialist army officers among its participants.

"However, let me make it clear that, despite those concrete facts, the CPS had not forged a systematic, general line to answer the main questions regarding the Salvadorean revolutionary struggle. The Party's official line cannot be said to have included, at that time, the course of armed struggle.

"But it is only fair to stress, in addition, that in the framework of a big upsurge in popular struggle in El Salvador, a struggle influenced by the historic victory of the Cuban revolution, the Central Committee unanimously passed, with the support of the entire Party, a guideline on preparing to take up arms.

"Between 1961 and 1963, the CPS built a mass movement to support the course of armed struggle of the Salvadorean revolution. In this connection, it should be pointed out that the CPS has always regarded armed struggle as a means of mass struggle. And so, the United Front for Revolutionary Action (FUAR) was founded.

"However, the Communist Party's efforts to implement armed struggle came up against a number of obstacles, largely due to the successful launching in 1962 of a process of dependent industrialization based on the Central American Common Market.

"Growth indexes reached high levels: 11 percent in industrial activity for several years; 12 to 13 percent in the Gross National Product. On this basis, the conditions changed for advancing towards higher stages of revolutionary struggle. The regime became consolidated, a limited democratic opening was launched, reforms were carried out in the electoral system and the electoral road gained validity in the eyes of the masses. Perhaps that was only apparent, but it was real enough to the masses at the time, and also to other parties, especially the Christian Democratic Party, founded in 1960, which began to chalk up a number of successes.

"The CPS then introduced tactical changes, without casting aside the thesis that armed struggle was the most likely course for taking power. This conviction was based on the analysis of the national situation, of the characteristics and peculiarities of class struggle in El Salvador, where a dictatorship which had been in power for decades, an oligarchy and in general, a recalcitrant, extremely repressive bourgeoisie, left no room for doubts.

"However, we found ourselves in a special situation: people needed to be won away from reformist conceptions, and the CPS found itself obliged to take part in the electoral process. Naturally, this meant that the CP worked hard to build a legal mechanism and join in open struggle. It mustn't be forgotten that, with the exception of the final months of 1931 when the Party took part in elections for mayor, it has been an illegal, underground party right from the start, and especially after the 1932 insurrection.

"And in the '60s the CP was the only revolutionary force in El Salvador and it simply could not turn its back on the electoral opening. The CP had to fight to win over the masses. In addition, we should stress all that the Party had to do, being illegal and underground and with the government knowing who was involved, to build a legal instrument. The only explanation is mass support for the CPS, its roots and its ties with the workers, students and intellectuals.

"And so, we took part in elections over a period of eleven years. From the start, we were well aware that the ballot box was not the way to take power, but we were also convinced that it was necessary to lead the people to learn for themselves, in the school of experience. From the end of 1966 to February 1977, we participated, alone or with other democratic organizations, in three presidential elections and six legislative or mayoral elections.

"The Salvadorean people and their candidates running on the ticket of the National Opposition Union (UNO) won the 1972 and 1977 presidential elections by a comfortable margin, but the ballot was not respected. However, the objective of our policy was to rally the democratic forces, and this was achieved with the formation of a united front. The regime was isolated

with its National Conciliation Party (PCN), a bureau-
cratic instrument with impositions from above, all
along the line.

"On two occasions it was demonstrated before the
masses that the road to power did not pass through the
ballot box. Higher forms of struggle had to be brought
into play. It would be necessary to take up arms."

**What was the CP's reaction to those rigged elec-
tions?**

"After the February 20, 1977 ballot-box fraud,
large-scale battles took place in the country. It was a
week of insurrections, and the CP played the role of the
principal leader in the eyes of the people. It was
precisely after those events that the majority of the
people began to support armed struggle.

"Then, the CPS also changed, with a Political Commission decision in April 1977. However, eleven years
of legal struggle and electoral participation had left
their mark upon us as well. Over 87 percent of the CPS
membership in February 1977 had joined the Party
during that period and had been educated in that form
of struggle. The time-honored Leninist thesis on the
need to be prepared for all forms of struggle to be able
to switch from one to another is not easy to apply, as
we certainly found out in practice.

"The ideological imprint left by those eleven years
upon the members and even the leadership of the CPS -
without exception - also stood in the way of a speedy,
effective change to higher forms of struggle. The Party
leadership had to make many a self-critical effort, and
it must be said that this is a constant throughout the
history of the Party. Beginning with the leadership, we
are a self-critical Party. And the self-critical effort of
the CPS leadership was crowned by our 7th Congress,
held underground, in April 1979.

"Two years behind the times, we took the step in the
direction of armed forms of struggle, which historically
had been placed on the agenda and no longer for the
revolutionaries alone, but for the masses of people."

How does the CPS interpret its armed struggle option?

"The CP's wholehearted incorporation in armed struggle, with the conviction that it is the only way to reach a real solution to the national crisis that will benefit the working people and the people in general, is neither an improvised act nor a last minute about-face: it is the expression of a long history of struggle.

"It is the result of a line set forth by the organization many years ago. But experience has shown that having a correct line is not enough. In addition, we needed to work very hard, to make a really concerted, solid effort to apply that line in practice, to be able to take the far-reaching step of leading the Party to engage in higher forms of class struggle.

"Armed struggle existed in El Salvador since before 1977, but I don't mean to say that we started at that moment. Ever since 1970, armed organizations appeared on the Salvadorean scene. However, those organizations were all, by and large, offshoots of the CPS, although there were other sources coming from radicalized Social Christian student sectors and even from the Christian Democratic Party itself. Moreover, the secretary general of the CPS, Salvador Cayetano Carpio, resigned from the leadership and from the Party itself to devote himself to the formation of the Farabundo Martí Popular Liberation Forces.

"When I place the stress on February 1977, it is because, once the electoral road was shut off, the broad masses of the people turned to armed struggle. Before that, the masses believed in the electoral road, otherwise there's no explaining the comfortable victory margin of UNO in the 1977 elections, a bigger victory than the one scored in 1972.

"Before that, it's true that the armed struggle organizations, some more than others, were chalking up successes in some areas, especially in certain rural zones that had undergone a drastic proletarianization process with the expansion of capitalism in farming. Those armed organizations enjoyed influence and important support bases in some rural areas, but at the same time their links with the workers in the cities and other areas of the country were weak. In general, up to February 1977, there was a great deal of confusion regarding armed struggle.

"Among people with good intentions, among working people, who at present are part of the revolutionary struggle, a common view was that guerrilla actions were organized by the enemy to justify the repression against the opposition forces.

"But after February 1977, those confusions ended. And that is another sign of what we call the general about-face which occurred among the majority of the people. During your travels around El Salvador, in the cities and in the countryside, you've probably seen how the vast majority of the people support the armed struggle. This, then, is the logic behind our decision. And I repeat, we recognize our errors and we recognize them publicly.

"Our Party is self-critical, and it is self-critical in public. Our decision to join wholeheartedly in armed struggle is a bit late, but still in time."

DIVISION WAS UNTENABLE

What about the prospects for further unity?

"The process will soon be capped by unifying all the people, all the revolutionary and democratic forces. The unity announcement gave rise to an outburst of popular rejoicing, which shows that division was untenable. The rank and file of all our organizations, the broad masses that are influenced by us, bore the burden of division as an unjustifiable evil. The burden had to be borne due to the discipline of the members of each organization. That's why the rejoicing was so incredible after the announcement of the establishment of the National Revolutionary Coordinating body. People hugged each other and expressed their solidarity in a very eloquent way.

"The division, however, has its historic explanation, not a justification, even though no one harbored ill intentions. Now, the most immediate antecedent, shall we say, that precipitated the Salvadorean unity agreement was the unity of the three currents comprising the Sandinista Front and which led to the victory of the Nicaraguan Revolution. Unity and victory, that necessary sequence in the triumph of the Nicaraguan people, made a strong impression in El Salvador, and the cause of unity became a banner for all.

"It can be said, and without exaggeration, that after the victory of the Nicaraguan Revolution, the cause of unity became a genuinely mass cause. The masses asked us: When are you going to get together, comrades? In reality, the mass pressure was considerable....Division was simply untenable."

A SINGLE PARTY OF THE REVOLUTION

"Now, we have a unity agreement that launched a process geared, in the view of the CPS, to the creation of a unified political-military revolutionary leadership and, moreover, to the creation of a single Marxist-Leninist party of the Salvadorean revolution.

"We're all working in that direction. We think that fighting shoulder to shoulder will unite us far more than undertaking a joint analysis of our country's problems, the problems of the revolution and its development. Shedding our blood in combat together unites us far more. A single revolutionary leadership can be expected in the near future, and the creation of a single party in the medium term."

"There is no possibility whatsoever for a reformist solution to the national crisis because there can be no holding back the revolutionary movement, deeply rooted in a people whose heroic struggle has developed under the savage blows of the oligarchy. The repressive machinery built up over half a century cannot be brought into line even with a bourgeois-democratic process. The Salvadorean oligarchy, and almost the entire bourgeoisie, with its deep, time-honored roots in land ownership and its Prussian ideology, frontally oppose far-reaching reforms and social transformations," Schafik Jorge Handal, general secretary of the Communist Party of Salvador told Prensa Latina in an exclusive interview.

In his analysis of the present stage of the Salvadorean process, he declared that, looking at this process through the prism of socialism, "the only genuinely revolutionary position for the CPS was to recognize, as a natural consequence of the late development of a dependent capitalist society, the plurality of the revolutionary organizations with a stable social base of their own in El Salvador; and to present the issue of the vanguard of the Salvadorean revolution as a problem to be solved on the basis of the unity of the revolutionary organizations, or what amounts to the same thing: a single vanguard is shaped in the process of progressive unification."

HISTORIC REASONS FOR DIVISION

What, in your opinion, are the causes of the divisions among the Salvadorean revolutionary organizations?

"That's an interesting question, because the unity issue is indissolubly linked with that of division and its causes. They are both part of a single process of development by way of contradictions. And since we delved deeply into the study of the causes and characteristics of the phenomena of division, we were prepared for unity.

"The CPS, as we indicated, was founded in 1930, while the groupings that gave rise to the revolutionary armed organizations did not come into being until 1970. This means that the CPS stood as a solitary fighter for the cause of the democratic revolution and socialism over the 40-year period. It was the only Marxist-Leninist organization in the country. It was combated by the enemy and for a long time was isolated from broad middle layers and even from sectors of workers. To give you some idea of the way things were for years in El Salvador, we Communists denied belonging to the Party in public. That was regarded as a serious accusation, and when we were charged with being Communists, we countered with the question: What about you, are you a cop?

"The masses of the people didn't realize that their struggles to back demands for improvements were being led by Communists. People were very prejudiced, and that led to some traumas among our own members, and also to some deviations in methods of work.

"Now, why did the CPS stand alone for so long? Unless this is analyzed in depth, it might be believed, to cite some superficial arguments, that it was because the CPS wielded some kind of monopoly over the left, failing to leave political space for anyone else. Or, that its political line was correct for 40 years but began to go wrong in 1970. That is: the revolutionary armed organizations arose ten years ago due to the CPS's errors and the fact that its monopoly over the left was untenable. We feel that the arguments contain some elements of truth, but certainly not the whole truth."

INDUSTRIALIZATION AND SOCIAL CHANGE

"In the '50s an industrialization process began in El Salvador that had been going on for 20 years in the countries of the southern cone of Latin America. The military dictatorship that took power after the defeat of the 1932 uprising consolidated the hegemonistic, absolute power of the coffee agro-export oligarchy. The state, the laws, government economic policy, the social structure, were all geared to benefit that oligarchy. Moreover, putting up factories in El Salvador was outlawed. It wasn't until after World War II and the coup by army majors in December 1948, that an industrialization process was able to begin, very gradually. Then, in the '60s, thanks to the Central American Common Market, it took on a faster pace. This was the period of penetration by big United States and Japanese corporations, especially the former.

"The industrialization process led to substantial changes in the class structure. Up to 1950 the working class was linked with workshops which were of an artisan nature because of the level of their technology and productive forces. There were few real factories in the country. Subsequently an industrial proletariat began to take shape. Its members were recruited in the countryside and in the towns of the hinterland. It was a proletariat without experience in class struggle; and so, a typical process of the dependent capitalist societies of Latin America was triggered off.

"This is a process in which large masses of people, especially those of rural origin, become a marginal population living in cities. At the same time, due to the needs of the industrialization process itself, the education system is expanded, with the concomitant appearance of a numerous sector of university students and intellectuals who, as is the case in all the dependent capitalist countries, comprise a mass which, to some extent, is also marginal. Its members cannot be absorbed by the industrial development process and, hence, they lack prospects in El Salvador.

"In 1963, for example, when the university reform movement was launched under CPS leadership in alliance with a prestigious group of intellectuals, the most outstanding of whom was Doctor Carlos Alfaro Castillo, there was just one university in the country, the state institution, with 3000 students.

"Now, in 1980, there are over 35,000 university students, and the rate of growth is higher than that of the industrial working class. Moreover, if to these sectors we add the industrial proletariat recruited in the countryside and resettled in the cities, and the people who, due to their numbers and technical qualifications, cannot be absorbed by the process of industrial expansion, then the phenomenon of the marginal masses takes on an extraordinary dimension.

"In addition, in the '60s and in the early '70s, dependent capitalism in El Salvador made considerable inroads into agriculture. Peasant farmers who rented land in exchange for payment in cash or kind were swept from the scene by modern capitalism which, as it gained the upper hand, proletarianized those people and implanted up-to-date techniques, geared to export.

"An upsurge of class struggle ensued. New conflicts cropped up, and so, that expansion of dependent capitalism in El Salvador contributed the social basis that made necessary the appearance of revolutionary organizations of different kinds. This is also the social base which provided the possibility for upholding different ideological and political shadings in the Salvadorean left.

"So, it was no accident that the beginnings of a crisis in the industrialization model based on the Central American Common Market, whose breakdown is closely linked with the 1969 war between El Salvador and Honduras, also precipitated what we regard as the mature phase of the structural crisis of dependent capitalism in our country. Or, that at the same time, the political scheme upheld by the CPS underwent a crisis, which was aggravated by the errors committed in connection with the war with Honduras."

MISTAKES OF THE 'EUROPEANS'

"The errors of the CPS acted as the detonator that gave rise to the other revolutionary organizations, but the deep roots, the causes, have a social and historical basis. In this process, the CPS analysis goes beyond the confrontation of ideological conceptions and the alleged monopoly of the revolutionary vanguard. It also feels that in the conditions of the social development of Latin America, the emergence of the working class and other social classes, groups and layers, as well as phenomena of different kinds, is decisively influenced and marked by the characteristics of dependent capitalism.

"Because of this, a sufficient social base exists for the appearance, not of one, but of several revolutionary organizations in a single country. Furthermore, while it is true that at first serious ideological differences arose and positions were taken up in the ideological struggle which, regarded in the light of the European experience, might be conceptualized under their specific names - ultraleftism, revisionism, etc. - the actual unfolding of the process has little by little made it plain that, although the ideological shadings do exist, with their concomitant doctrinal positions, at bottom, it is not the same. The results have not been engendered by identical causes.

"In addition, although the same classes are involved, they do not have the same characteristic as in classical, independent capitalist development. Because of this, and precisely because of this, those revolutionary currents in the dependent capitalist countries of Latin America are lasting ones. They are not affected by the infantile disorder of ultraleftism that is overcome with the maturity of the working class parties. No: these currents appear time and time again, they receive defeat after defeat, only to appear all over again, because they have a stable, developing and expanding social base."

THE PROBLEM OF THE VANGUARD

"Therefore, we reached the conclusion that the only genuinely revolutionary position for the CPS was to recognize, as a natural consequence of the late development of a dependent capitalist society, the plurality of the revolutionary organizations with a stable social base of their own in El Salvador, and present the issue of the vanguard of the Salvadorean revolution as a problem to be solved on the basis of the unity of the revolutionary organizations, or what amounts to the same thing: a single vanguard is shaped in the process of growing unity.

"Those are the foundations of our unity policy, of our line on the unity of the revolutionary forces."

CRISIS OF THE SOCIAL FORMATION AS A WHOLE

What is the CP's opinion of the present ruling junta?

"This is a second attempt. There is no possibility whatsoever for a reformist solution to the national crisis. And these are the reasons why it is out of question: first of all, because there can be no holding back the revolutionary movement, deeply rooted in a people whose heroic struggle has unfolded under the savage blows of the oligarchy.

"Secondly, because the machinery of repression built up over half a century cannot be brought into line even with a democratic-bourgeois process. That machinery is complex and involves not only the armed forces but thousands of persons who have been trained to place their intelligence at the service of the counter-revolution, to torture and murder the people. Without destroying that machinery, there can be no process of real democratization.

"And a reformist solution demands, precisely, answers to two problems: democratization and structural changes by way of reforms. But El Salvador is undergoing not only a crisis of its political system but a deep-going structural crisis, a crisis of the socio-economic formation as a whole.

"Thirdly, because the Salvadorean oligarchy and almost the entire bourgeoisie, with its deep, time-honored roots in land ownership and its Prussian ideology, totally oppose deep-going reforms and social transformations.

"So, none of the three points could be solved by way of reforms and evolution. Revolution is the only course."

UNITY MUST BE BROAD TO WIN

Then, why did the CPS take part in the first ruling junta after the overthrow of General Carlos Humberto Romero in October 1979?

"The CPS took part because the Salvadorean revolution also needs the democratic forces. The revolutionary movement alone cannot win. And at that time, after the fall of the regime of General Romero, the democratic currents, the progressive sectors, offered their support and joined the ruling junta.

"And, since the CPS was the revolutionary organization with the oldest ties with the democratic forces, with which it had earlier conducted a policy of alliances, it had to accompany those forces, stand beside them until the project met with failure in order to prevent their dispersion after defeat and be able immediately to link them up with the revolutionary movement.

"And in the second place, notwithstanding the fact that the October 15, 1979 coup was a maneuver by imperialism and the Salvadorean right wing, there was involved in it a patriotic, progressive current of young army officers who were unaware of the objectives of our main enemy and who in fact had placed their hopes on such a solution to the national crisis.

"Now, the roads are defined, for their officers as well. It is historically possible for part of the army to join the people and their revolutionary movement. The CPS feels that this is a fine possibility, but it also stresses that the revolution is an irreversible process whose victory does not depend on whether or not part of the army takes part.

"However, it is also true that the incorporation of the patriotic officers would mean a savings in terms of social cost, and we revolutionaries are the first to try to avoid violence and its tragic consequences. Reaction, for its part, is trying to claim that we Communists are infiltrating and involved in a plot to split the army. That is totally false. What is happening, however, is that the soldiers of the Salvadorean army are mainly peasants, rural laborers, workers, while the officers and non-coms are from the various middle sectors, and all of them are involved in the process taking place in the country.

"Hence, despite the institutional blocks, the deformation of the reactionary command and United States influence, the generalized, heroic struggle of the Salvadorean people, of which the soldiers are a part, is necessarily reflected in the garrisons. Those officers and soldiers are aware of the urgent need for radical changes, and the CPS feels that they need to take their own course and learn from experience, so that they themselves will come to the conclusion that there is only one way to provide a real solution to the country's problems, the revolution.

"In addition, in regard to our participation in the first ruling junta, it must be emphasized that the CPS did not limit itself to a presence, shall we say, of personalities. No: it was the only political force that released a platform and a program for political and structural changes in keeping with the popular interests. And that program, albeit mutilated, is the one the second junta is using to try to stay in power. Let me stress the word mutilated, because the political changes designed to expel the fascists from the state apparatus were not carried out.

"Nor did the repression cease, nor were political prisoners released. The killers and torturers were not punished, the paramilitary bodies were not liquidated and all that has already given rise to a fresh crisis.

"The first ruling junta failed, as the CPS expected, and that was a defeat for the fascists because the democratic forces meted out telling blows as they withdrew. So, for imperialism, the oligarchy and their allies, the only realistic option is fascism, fascist counterrevolution, the destruction of the Salvadorean revolution, but this has already become impossible. In antagonistic contradiction to that is the other realistic, historic option: the armed revolutionary option.

"Moreover, despite the fact that the Christian Democrats are present in the ruling junta, it must be noted that within that party there are progressive currents, and as the class struggle sharpens, they will join the people, the revolutionary movement, which does not close its doors to them."

THE MNR IS WITH THE PEOPLE

What is the CP opinion of the Social Democrats?

"In El Salvador, Social Democracy finds concrete expression in the National Revolutionary Movement (MNR) which two years ago joined the Socialist International. This is a party that groups a sector of prestigious intellectuals who consistently stand with the people's cause. Despite its membership in the Socialist International, the MNR upholds its advanced positions, its commitment to the Salvadorean people's movement.

"Moreover, for the past ten years, the CPS and the MNR have been taking part together in the political process; we've covered the same road. And although this is not the time for analyzing the Socialist International, which contains different currents, it should be stressed that in Latin America, Social Democracy follows an antifascist policy in defense of human rights and freedoms."

"We have entered the final stage, the homestretch, the period of large-scale battles for power," Schafik Jorge Handal, general secretary of the Communist Party of El Salvador, told Prensa Latina in an exclusive interview.

He added:

"The Salvadorean revolution is democratic and anti-imperialist because its fundamental goals are freedom and respect for human rights, a deep-going agrarian reform that will conclusively solve the problem of the countryside, and authentic national independence."

The picture brings to mind Nicaragua in October 1977....

"We're not talking about a directly socialist revolution; however, because independent capitalism is historically impossible in our country, and we think in the rest of Latin America as well, and because power will be wielded by the great majority of the people, democratic, anti-imperialist tasks and objectives will thus become the first phase of a single revolution, which is esentially socialist in nature." Handal has a frank way of speaking and leaves no room for confusion. In political practice, this has certainly paid, enabling the CPS to forge solid and lasting alliances with organizations such as the social democratic National Revolutionary Movement (MNR) which has always been familiar with the politics, goals and forms of struggle of the Communist Party, which it regards as a "consistent ally."

REVOLUTIONS ARE NOT IMPLANTED BY DECREE

What is the strategy of the CPS and what are its immediate goals?

"The CPS's strategy is inscribed in the context of the democratic, anti-imperialist revolution and in the option of armed struggle for taking power which will come about with the unity of action of the revolutionary and democratic forces.

"So, we aren't talking about a directly socialist revolution. Revolutions are not imposed by some decree issued by a force aiming to speed up the historic process. Our revolution will take place because it meets the objective reality of El Salvador. The democratic, anti-imperialist revolution in our country is in correspondence with a dependent capitalist society with middling development in comparison with other dependent capitalist nations.

"The CPS established three basic tasks and objectives for the Salvadorean revolution: first, freedom and respect for human rights, because for the past half a century a military dictatorship has held power, and it has been growing more and more repressive and savage; second, a deep-going agrarian reform that will make the people who work the land the owners of that land and its produce, in order to provide a conclusive solution to the problems of the countryside; third, authentic national independence, the need for which is not so evident today for the large majority of people as are the first two goals. However as the process advances and imperialism strives to hold it back, this objective too will become clear to the people and will turn into a strong motivation. National independence has a series of economic, political, ideological and cultural implications. Without achieving it, it is impossible to come up with real solutions to El Salvador's general crisis, stigmatized by dependence."

MAIN PROBLEM OF THE REVOLUTION

 In the present international situation, does the CPS feel that those democratic, anti-imperialist tasks and objectives can be achieved without heading for socialism?

"No, that's impossible. For one thing, the main problem of the revolution is the problem of power. With victory, the great majority of the people - the working class in general, the peasants, the middle layers - destroy the old machinery of repression and set up revolutionary power.

"Then, democratic, anti-imperialist tasks and objectives become the first phase of a single revolution, which in the final analysis is in essence socialist."

How long does one phase last and how do you go from one to the other?

"That can't be answered ahead of time. It's connected with concrete national and international conditions that serve as the setting for the revolutionary victory. The main thing is for the Salvadorean revolutionaries to take power and launch the process of change, with a vanguard strong enough to keep up the pace of that process of change, that is, a pace in keeping with the interests of the people and the defense and advance of the revolution.

"That phase may be brief or protracted, violent or relatively peaceful. In Cuba, for example, the defense of the revolution called for a rapid transition to socialism. In Nicaragua, it remains to be seen. Such things can't be decreed; much less are solutions possible ahead of time or in the abstract.

"So, the CPS asserts that the Salvadorean revolution is democratic and anti-imperialist, and this is what makes it possible to organize a broad front not only of revolutionary but also of democratic forces. Each force heads for its objectives with its program. Along the way, it tries to influence the historic process, and this is legitimate. We are sincere in our formulation. The CPS isn't out to trick anyone or lead the democratic forces into some kind of trap. In fact, stating this is an insult to the groups of talented, politically able people who lead the democratic forces and are perfectly aware of the relationship between democratic and socialist revolutions."

INDEPENDENT CAPITALISM OUT OF THE QUESTION IN LATIN AMERICA

What is the CPS's attitude to the Salvadorean bourgeoisie?

"When the CPS speaks of the driving forces of the Salvadorean revolution, it does not include any sector of the bourgeoisie. However, we do think that some individuals or groups, or even sectors, at a given moment could adopt an attitude in favor of the process.

"This policy is in line with a CPS thesis that independent capitalism is now historically impossible in El Salvador, and we think that in Latin America as well. Therefore, no sector of the bourgeoisie, because of its condition, nature and class essence, can carry out and be consistent with the anti-imperialist tasks which, in the long run, determine the fate of the revolution and its democratic objectives.

"There can be no real democracy for the majority of the Salvadorean masses, nor can there be an effective solution to the problems of the land, in the framework of dependency. No dependent capitalist country can be a model for solving those problems. So, there is no bourgeois sector that can consistently confront imperialism, because there is no longer any possibility for independent capitalism.

"The only possible capitalism is capitalism dependent upon imperialism, under one form or another. There is a very big difference between this situation and the role of the national bourgeoisie in the colonies.

"This is linked with the progress of class formation, which has been different in the colonies and in Latin America. In our countries there is no issue about whether or not capitalism will win out, because what already exists is dependent capitalist society, and this is the type of society that is in crisis, not the precapitalist vestiges.

"In El Salvador, what has reached a crisis is the entire structure of dependent capitalist society. Without solving that structural crisis, there can be no real solution for the problems of a democratic nature. At present, with a revolutionary situation ripening and the crisis sharpening to an extreme degree, the bourgeoisie is splitting apart, and there are sectors which, for the sake of finding a way out or a way to rule, may at a given point adopt a position in favor of revolution.

"In Nicaragua this was very evident. The CPS feels that this has nothing to do with the historic role and attitude of the bourgeoisie in, and in regard to, the revolution. It is, instead, the result of the political crisis inherent in a revolutionary situation."

DEEPENING INTERNATIONALISM

What is the CPS's international policy?

"Our Party....regards imperialism as the main enemy. Thus, our international policy is for world peace, detente, the peoples' struggle for social liberation and against all forms of oppression and exploitation. The CPS stands in solidarity with Vietnam, Kampuchea and Laos and condemns the criminal, traitorous and divisive activity of the leadership of the Government and misnamed Communist Party of China. It supports the Movement of Non-Aligned Countries, and identifies with the Cuban Revolution, whose defense is also a matter of principal.

"But in addition to this international position, the CPS decidedly supports unity of action between the Communist Parties and all the revolutionary organizations that are struggling in Latin America, just as it has in El Salvador.

"The CPS feels that the Latin American communist movement has no monopoly of the revolutionary vanguard and that the latter must emerge in the unity process of the revolutionary organizations.

"Moreover, proletarian internationalism must not be limited to the denunciation of repression and to solidarity with political prisoners, the tortured and the persecuted. Instead, it must deepen its revolutionary awareness and find expression in solidarity for the offensive in the struggle for the victory of the revolution, until there is blood unity in Africa, Asia and Latin America. The Nicaraguan Revolution enabled us to manifest that solidarity on the offensive, and now all Central America is becoming a suitable setting for further enhancing the revolutionary essence of proletarian internationalism."

EL SALVADOR ENTERS THE HOMESTRETCH

▌▌ How does the CPS see El Salvador's immediate future?

"Without question, this is the year of great upsurge in revolutionary struggle.

"Unity doesn't just add, it multiplies. The alliance of the revolutionary and democratic forces generates vast social energy and while we can't give any guarantees that victory will take place in the next few months, we can say that we've entered the homestretch, the period of large-scale battles for power.

"A comparison with the Nicaraguan process helps to explain the Salvadorean situation today. I think it's legitimate to place the start of the final stage in October 1977, when the Sandinista National Liberation Front (FSLN) began a series of attacks at the occupation of military garrisons and strongholds.

"Between October 1977 and July 1979, a historically brief period was covered, but in the process there were advances and reverses. There were large-scale general strikes and there was the extraordinary insurrection of September 1978, which was not crowned with victory. There was the withdrawal, but also a counter-offensive to achieve victory, combining general popular insurrection, guerrilla warfare, a war of movement and positions, with the participation of hundreds of thousands of Nicaraguans, especially young people, and a big internationalist effort, with the support of progressive peoples and governments.

"The period in El Salvador may be protracted or brief. But we've entered the last phase, we're on the homestretch."

VI
With the
Party of
National Resistance
(FARN)

FERMAN CIENFUEGOS

Last call to the military

"It is time for those honorable and patriotic young officers found in the heart of the reactionary armed forces to come take up their positions in the popular revolutionary movement. It is time to abandon immediately the fascist leaders who have now intensified the massive assassination of the Salvadorean people to protect the interests of the oligarchy and imperialism," the secretary general of the National Resistance Party and high commander of the Armed Forces of National Resistance, Ernesto Jovel,* told Prensa Latina in an exclusive interview.

Next to the industrial textile worker were other young members of the National Executive Directors, tempered in the heat of adversity, whose lives reflect the history of the politico-military organization; the second-in-command and ex-university student Fermán Cienfuegos, and the worker Julia Rodríguez.

ORIGINS OF THE NATIONAL RESISTANCE

The National Resistance is the result of self-sacrificing work begun by a small and experienced group of working class youths and students, who came together in 1975 as an independent organization of the People's Revolutionary Army (ERP), pledging themselves to an effort of identifying with the dispossessed, taking up the difficult task of building a party with its military structure - militia, guerrilla, army - and its mass front, with the goal of successfully struggling against the military dictatorship of the fourteen families which are supported by the U.S. government.

After five years of following a difficult course that has demanded much sacrifice and blood, the National Resistance today exercises a significant influence in the heart of the working class, in broad sectors and popular organizations and, together with the Communist Party of El Salvador, the Popular Liberation Forces "Farabundo Martí," and the Revolutionary Party of El Salvador/Revolutionary Army of the People, is ready to "crush the fascists."

Ernesto Jovel says:

"We hold the position that the vanguard exists in several tendencies....and the Party seeks it out in many places. It had to unite to make revolution and take power. From this we had to begin to build three tools: the Party, as a strategic and tactical leadership nucleus, the Mass Front, to unite all the popular forces in a political army against a common enemy, and the Armed Revolutionary Forces as the military tool to destroy the reactionary forces. The Party with unified leadership directs both political and military fields.

DEMOCRATIC REVOLUTIONARY GOVERNMENT

What is the strategy of the National Resistance and what are the immediate objectives within reach of the armed force?

Fermán Cienfuegos replies:

"The objective of the current stage of the struggle is the seizure of power and the establishment of a government of workers and peasants, in alliance with the middle class, which means it will be a democratic and revolutionary government, sustained by the Revolutionary and Democratic forces....Several problems come up in our strategy....One of these, that of Party unity, has been changed into a tactical problem due to the unity established in the National Revolutionary Coordinator. We believe that the process of unification of the disparate tendencies of yesterday begins to concretize, to translate into the reality of concrete acts, the unified vanguard of the Salvadorean revolution....

"As for the problem of constructing the Armed Revolutionary Forces, we also believe that fundamental steps have been made....One of these is the Popular Army, in a heightened process of formation, another is the arming of the Salvadorean masses....Several years ago, the arming of the masses was a theoretical problem and today it is a problem that is resolved in practice....In this manner, the strategic and immediate join, bind together....For another thing, we used to consider that the unity of the Popular Movement was a strategic problem, but the Mass Revolutionary Coordinator, which joins together the main mass organizations, reduces the problem to an immediate task.... So, in this sense, to repeat, we consider that, due to the advances gained, the strategic points have become the order of the day and are problems for immediate disposition. This reflects, in part, the maturation of the democratic and revolutionary government that is starting to take shape in concrete form....It will be the tool used to build the new society: without misery, or illiteracy or disease. A just and peaceful society, built for all Salvadoreans. This society will be the coming together once again of the people of El Salvador and their own country, and will be built by the process of the popular democratic revolution during the period of the transition to socialism.

THE HOUR OF THE PEOPLE HAS ARRIVED

 What perspective does the National Resistance have on the alliance between the military and the Christian Democrats?

Julia Rodríguez, the young woman with skin tanned by the sun of the cotton and corn fields, offers the answer:

"This alliance constitutes the second emergency government that imperialism and the oligarchy have used in a fruitless attempt to find a way out of the national crisis and to avoid the transfer of power to the hands of the Salvadorean people.

"Its duration will depend on the revolutionary and democratic forces, and we consider the hour of the people to have arrived, the hour when power will be in the people's hands."

And do you consider that there is no possibility of a peaceful solution to the current problems?

Fermán Cienfuegos, second-in-command of the political-military organization, replies:

"We want peace and a fair resolution of the national problems. Those who don't want peace, nor a solution to the problems that would benefit the working people, are the oligarchy and the guardian of their riches, imperialism, which is embedded wherever it pleases: in the reactionary Armed Forces, in the government, all over....The people have tried for all peaceful outcomes, have exhausted the established channels of the constitution, and the answer that has been received has been that of cruel repression. Now nothing is left but the armed road to win social liberation."

THE MILITARY AND THE CHURCH

Doesn't the National Resistance place some sort of hope in a particular sector of the government armed forces?

Ernesto Jovel, top leader of the FARN, says:

"In the heart of the reactionary Armed Forces there is a sector of honorable and patriotic young officers whom, through the Prensa Latina, we exhort to immediately abandon the fascist rulers, who have now intensified the massive assassination of the working people of El Salvador to protect the interests of the oligarchy and imperialism. It is time that this democratic sector come take up the corresponding positions in the popular revolutionary movement. This is the last chance, because the compromises they now make with the fascists take on an irreversible character."

And what is the political line of the National Resistance in relation to the Church?

The Secretary General of the Party says:
"Our political line on the Church is clear, exact, and definite: we respect religious freedom, cultural freedom. And, in a special way, we consider that the church of the poor, the church represented by the Archbishop of San Salvador, Monsignor Oscar Arnulfo Romero, plays a progressive and brave role in the struggle of the people, and has its place in the democratic Salvadorean revolution. Yes, definitely, this church will have to share with us many of the tasks in the process of the democratic revolution...."

IT IS SALVADOREAN

In regard to the revolutionary process, the forces of international reaction invariably say that the leadership, the economic and logistic support, the training of insurgents, etc., come from countries where they are building socialism. What does the National Resistance think of this?

Julia Rodríguez states:
"Our own revolution is Salvadorean, very much our own: no one comes to tell us what we should do or how or when we should do it....Nevertheless, this doesn't mean that we reject the experience of other people who today are masters of their destiny, to the contrary: we try to learn from others' experience....and we identify with the struggles of all oppressed and exploited, particularly the kinds of struggles of our fellow peoples of Central America....This internal independence is necessarily reflected in international politics and so we also identify with the Non-Aligned Movement and with democratic governments like Mexico, Costa Rica, Panama and members of the Andean Pact, all of whom took

WITH THE PARTY OF NATIONAL RESISTANCE

anti-imperialist positions and prevented U.S. intervention in Nicaragua....We are sure that this same solidarity will be offered to El Salvador, where North American military intervention is a fact...."

VIETNAM BEGAN LIKE THIS

"No efforts have been spared in seeking a way out of the national political and economic crisis. We try by all means to avoid a bloodbath in the country, but all the established channels have been closed off to the Salvadorean people, all paths and also patience have been exhausted. We have been obliged to go on to the higher stage of armed struggle, and we are prepared for massive confrontation," Ernesto Jovel, the top leader of the National Resistance, told Prensa Latina.

"Right now, a call for a general uprising would immediately bring 100,000 Salvadoreans into the struggle, and the number would triple in the following days...." added Fermán Cienfuegos, the second-in-command of the political-military organization.

Meanwhile, numerous North American officials, situated in the major districts of the country, direct the reactionary Salvadorean armed forces in operations with a clear and definite objective: to destroy the people in the rural area where the organizations of the Popular Revolutionary Bloc, the "February 28th" People's League, the Democratic National Union, and the Popular United Action Front are found, that is, the members of the Mass Revolutionary Coordinator.

Precisely as part of the "war of extermination," the Center for Engineering Instruction for the Armed Forces (CIFA), located in the city of Zacatecoluca in the department of La Paz, in the center of the nation, has been transformed by the U.S. advisors into a strategic base with helicopters, tanks, and various types of armed vehicles, heavy artillery and special troops which, in recent times, razed the cantons of Suchitoto and wide areas of Chalatenango, San Vicente and Cojutepeque, among others. The incendiary bombs, deadly chemicals, and machine guns have caused hundreds of deaths and injuries.

This is also how the U.S. began its involvement in

the war in Viet Nam in Southeast Asia.

GUATEMALA: CENTER OF REACTION

It is no secret that the government, the army, and the paramilitary groups of the Guatemalan extreme right actively support their counterparts in El Salvador.

In Guatemala, today converted by the United States and Israel into the center for counterrevolution in Central America, are found the main bases for logistical support, training, and staging of mercenaries to fight against the people's movement in El Salvador.

Ex-members of the Somocista National Guard, North Americans, counterrevolutionaries, Cubans, and members of the fascist National Democratic Organization (ORDEN) are trained by specialists in counterinsurgency warfare from the United States, Israel, and the old corrupt Saigon.

The military-industrial complex Israel Aircraft Industries has an attractive market in Guatemala, El Salvador, and Honduras, whose governments have acquired numerous Arava-201 and several Mystere aircraft, Dabur patrol boats with Gabriel computer-controlled rockets, Galil and M-16 rifles and Uzi submachine guns, several hundred long range cannon and mortars, armed transport vehicles and various armaments for tens of millions of dollars.

At the western port of Acajutla, in the department of Sonsonate, Israeli ships arrive abundantly loaded with arms for the repressive forces of El Salvador, and with Israeli instructors whose role is to train the Salvadorean National Guard.

The United States, for its part, is increasing and speeding up the sending of advisors and arms of all types to the Central American military regimes. The Honduran government of General Policarpo Paz García serves as the intermediary for the buying and selling of war materials between the North American corporations - such as that over which General Alexander Haig, ex-commander of the North Atlantic Treaty Organization (NATO) presides - and the National Private Enterprises Association (ANEP) of El Salvador, headed by Eduardo Palomo.

At the same time on the southern coast of Guatemala, on the "African" Hacienda, property of the family of Colonel Miguel Angel Ponciano, located on the border with El Salvador, in San José Acatempa in the department of Jutiapa, strong contingents of mercenaries are currently being trained.

And Ponciano and Sandoval Alarcón, heads of the ultraright "national liberation" movement and the institutionalized bands of Guatemala assasins, maintain close relations with general José Alberto Medrano and Major Roberto D'Abuisson, the leaders of ORDEN.

A NEW ARMY OF MERCENARIES

The United States directs the intervention in El Salvador from Guatemala and Venezuela, because its objective is not limited to the homeland of Agustín Farabundo Martí, but rather extends to Nicaragua.

In the present stage, the Pentagon, the large transnational corporations, and the most reactionary sectors of Christian Democracy, in conjunction with the oligarchies and the Central American Defense Council (CONDECA), believe that the process of social liberation which is rapidly developing in Central America must be stopped "with fire and blood" in El Salvador and in Guatemala, and turned around in the land of the immortal Augusto César Sandino.

Due to this, the realistic and foresighted sector of the Christian Democratic Party of El Salvador renounced that political body and chose the path of exile.

Meanwhile, the right-wing sector presided over by José Napoleón Duarte strengthens its links with the fourteen families and the guardians of its riches, and enlists the aid of its counterparts in the Venezuelan Christian Democrats in its projects of "massacres and reforms," who support them with arms, money, advisors, and the formation of another army of mercenaries opposed to the Farabundo Martí Popular Liberation Forces, the Communist Party of El Salvador, the National Resistance, the Salvadorean Revolutionary Party/People's Revolutionary Army; Puerto Rican and Venezuelan soldiers make up the majority of these mercenary forces which prepare to attack the Central American insurgents from the south The Venezuelan General Hilarión Carza is one of those in charge of coordinating the plans with the Minister of Defense and Public Safety of El Salvador, Colonel José Guillermo García. **

STRUCTURES OF THE NATIONAL RESISTANCE

At what stage of development is the National Resistance?

Ernesto Jovel, the leader of the political-military revolutionary organization, offers this reply:

"The current structure of the National Resistance Party serves as an indicator of our development....The highest body of political and military leadership is the Delegates' Council - something like a congress - made up of the most advanced militants of the whole country....The Delegates' Council is headed up by the Secretary General of the Party and the second-in-command, who, in turn, make up the general military command, and so the political and the military are joined in this way....In this top executive structure there are also a certain number of comrades who are in charge of the work of organization, the masses, the use of the military, propaganda, ideological development, international relations, and other specific tasks, including agitation....

"For another thing, the National Resistance has something called the 'Broadened Leadership,' a non-statutory body that was formed to help with internal democracy of the party and the difficult job of bringing together the council delegates when they need to solve problems they have in common. This has served to make discussion more active and to come up with efficient answers in the political arena....The 'Broadened Leadership' thus acts as a consulting body, not a decision-making one, for the National Executive Direction....

"The National Resistance operates in regions, and each has its own leadership which takes up and elaborates the work of the sectors, including the workers, the peasants, and the middle classes. Each one has a coordinator, and each coordinator has its own cell units making up its structure, and these send roots into the midst of the people....The cell units maintain the lines of communication between the Party and the masses."

█▌ And the Revolutionary Armed Forces?

Fermán Cienfuegos gives the answer:

"Well, we have built the Armed Forces of the National Resistance on top of the structural base of the Party....This means that the military structure is tied, intersects, and occasionally is parallel to the Party structure. This is clear when we note that objective fact: many militants have military roles. After all, we must not forget that El Salvador is a country at war....

"The structure of the Armed Forces of National Resistance (FARN) is as follows: the General Military Command, made up of Ernesto Jovel and Fermán Cienfuegos, leads the High Command at the national scale and each region has its own High Command, in whose center, according to the division of labor, is the operative or military commission, responsible for the guerrilla and the militia....As far as the militia is concerned, the National Resistance works in columns, each one with a total of 50 combatants, and those, in turn, act in squads. There are five squads in each column....The masses, for their part, have created their own armed self-defense brigades to protect the demonstrations, political meetings, and whatever other people's activity....

"In our country the political movement of the masses is armed, because the people are firmly and irrevocably determined to defend themselves in the face of the permanent aggression....The Salvadorean people, then, are a people in arms....The FARN militias actively fight at the side of the people: it is somewhat like an irregular army, at times complementary to the guerrilla, and at times acting like shock troops and a vanguard....The guerrilla is our basic unit operating in the sector, and is made up of 25 combatants....and the FARN has carried out urban military operations involving between 150 and 200 comrades....For example: in September 1979 we occupied the cities of Soyapango, Armenia, and El Tránsito, with 40,000, 15,000 and 10,000 inhabitants respectively...."

AN INSURRECTIONAL METHOD IS ADOPTED

 What objectives does the National Resistance pursue with the military occupation of various types of towns?

Ernesto Jovel, the industrial textile worker, says:

"The fundamental objective is to prepare the masses for their incorporation into a process of insurrection....

"When a city, a town, a hacienda, a cottage, etc., is occupied, we inspire confidence in the people, who open their doors and houses, and firmly and enthusiastically help assure the maximal development and success of the operation....During the time we are there, we teach them about the political-military organization and how to operate and manufacture arms....In the face of the oligarchy's corrupt and compromised press, we take on the role of a true information source, and we explain the general situation and clarify doubts....

"The people are convinced that the only road left to gain true social liberation is the armed one, and because of this there is an armed mass movement that, in heightened form, acquires superior technique and discipline....The moment of insurrection has arrived, but we want international public opinion to be convinced that we took recourse in the armed struggle in our country because there were no other roads left....No efforts are spared to seek a political and social way out of the national crisis. We try by all means to avoid a general bloodbath in the country, but all channels within the system have been closed to the Salvadorean people, and all paths and patience have been exhausted....They have forced us to move to a higher stage of the armed struggle and we are prepared for a massive confrontation."

▌▌ And what is the opinion of the National Resistance on this massive confrontation?

Fermán Cienfuegos observes:

"Right now, a call from the Revolutionary Coordinator to general insurrection would mean the immediate incorporation of a hundred thousand Salvadoreans into the armed struggle and the number would triple in the following days....The military occupations that we have carried out in the past few months have demonstrated this, revolutionary occupations that have also served to temper our combatants and to show the enemy that the people can count on their own military forces."

REAL PEOPLE'S POWER

▌▌ You have spoken of the Revolutionary Coordinator. What are the prospects for unity between the revolutionary and democratic forces in El Salvador?

The second-in-command of the National Resistance explains:

"Without unity, we cannot be victorious....And that which we have gained now will result in future people's power....It is worth saying: the broad unity of the popular movement will be concretized in a real power of the Salvadorean people, a power that is within our reach and that will guide the destiny of the country."

---

* On September 20, 1980 Ernesto Jovel lost his life in a plane crash.

** Since this interview was first published certain events have occurred which seem to indicate that Venezuela may have modified its support of U.S. policy.

VII
With the
Popular
Revolutionary Bloc
(BPR)

FRANK MANUELO

JUAN CHACON

The Salvadorean people have won the political battle

"The people have won the political battle, and the conditions for general victory exist. But the dilemma of revolution or death is constant and even more so in the coming weeks, which will be decisive for the process of social liberation. Objectively, the Salvadorean masses are unable to withstand multinational armed foreign intervention, prepared and directed by the United States Government," said Juan Chacón, general secretary of the Popular Revolutionary Bloc (BPR), in an exclusive interview with Prensa Latina*.

The top leader of the most powerful mass organization in this small country at war, whose "death" was reported a few days ago by none other than the U.S. Ambassador Robert White, said that the "imperialist program which takes expression through the fascistic junta has been defeated by the organized, combative people, a people who in spite of the state of seige and virtual martial law, mobilize to take action, as shown after the barbaric and cowardly murder of Monsignor Oscar Arnulfo Romero."

CRIMINALS ISOLATED

This 24-year-old former shoeshine boy and farm worker told us that the top military brass and the most reactionary wing of Christian Democracy "are totally

---

* Juan Chacon, and five other leaders of the Democratic Revolutionary Front (FDR), were assassinated by government security forces on November 27, 1980.

isolated, cornered and demoralized. And the situation in which they find themselves 'explains' the brutal crime that has shaken the whole world with indignation and horror....The fascists had two goals in mind when they murdered the archbishop of San Salvador: to intimidate the masses and show that they were and are ready to do anything to defend the interests of the fourteen families and imperialism, whose interests are their own. However, the outcome was the opposite: the Salvadorean people demonstrated their organizational and political capability, responding with an eight-day general strike that paralyzed the economy of the country; carried out numerous operations in town and countryside; and, in military terms, the revolutionary organizations registered notable gains....It is clear that the Farabundo Martí Popular Liberation Forces, the National Resistance, the Communist Party and the Party of the Salvadorean Revolution-People's Revolutionary Army have the support of the masses, because the masses realize that in our country revolutionary violence is the only way to win power."

How does the Popular Revolutionary Bloc view the Salvadorean Democratic Front?

Juan, son of Felipe de Jesús Chacón, who was brutally murdered on August 26, 1977 - found shot in the head, his face skinned, his eyes gouged and his tongue cut off - for implementing the social doctrine of the Catholic Church; the son of this outstanding member of the Movement for Christianity Courses and good friend of Monsignor Oscar Arnulfo Romero, told us:

"The Salvadorean Democratic Front (FDS), which came into being on April 2 this year, shows that the military junta imposed by Washington and the Christian Democrats led by José Napoleón Duarte lack support and have no political alternatives to continue their domination. Imperialism, the oligarchy and their allies are isolated....The FDS, on the other hand, is made up of several labor federations with more than 50,000 members, the Independent Movement of Professionals and Technicians, the Social Democratic Party and an

important breakaway group from the Christian Democrats who split when the party decided to back the
junta, its policy of repression and its promises of
reforms. The FDS has endorsed the program of the
Revolutionary Mass Coordinating body made up of the
Unitary Popular Action Front (FAPU), Democratic National Union (UDN), 28th of February Popular Leagues
and Popular Revolutionary Bloc*. The active support of
democratic sectors for the struggle to end exploitation
and repression strengthens the unity of the popular
movement, gives added vigor to the process of liberation and corners and demoralizes the enemies of the
Salvadorean people who are internationally repudiated
for their policy of genocide."

U.S. AT A DEAD END

How does the Popular Revolutionary Bloc think
the United States will react to the evident failure
of its political program in El Salvador?

Chacón, who heads a 100,000-strong organization,
told us:

"It is clear that there are no prospects for U.S.
domination in our country, where all its plans have been
foiled, defeated by the organized, combative people.
Nor does it have any prospects in Central America
following the victory of the Nicaragua Revolution,
which halted its economic, political, military and social
domination. However, we must be realistic, precisely
because U.S. imperialism knows that the loss of El
Salvador will mean the loss of Guatemala and Honduras
and will help bring an end to its strategy of regional
domination; because of this, we repeat, it will not
hesitate for one moment in furthering the scope of
intervention, in a drive to destroy the revolutionary
organizations and end mass insurgency. We must see
things as they are....First, the United States could use
the army of mercenaries it has prepared in Guatemala,

---

* On April 18, 1980, the FDS and the Revolutionary Mass Coordinator
(CRM) united to form the Democratic Revolutionary Front (FDR).

Honduras, and other countries of the continent, an army which would be backed by the puppet forces of Guatemala and Honduras....It could also resort to an Inter-American 'peace-keeping force' to stop the 'communist threat'....And as a last resort, it could act directly, as in the Dominican Republic, on a mass scale, with its special operational divisions now stationed in the Caribbean....We must also point out, continuing in the same objective vein, that the people of El Salvador could not withstand multinational armed intervention on their own and this intervention would be linked to an attack on Nicaragua....But Salvadorean revolutionaries know that such a barbaric act would be opposed in various ways, in line with the possibilities open to each of the world's peoples."

BPR IS NOT A POLITICAL PARTY

Abroad there is considerable confusion about the specific nature and functions of the BPR. It is sometimes described almost as if it were a political party participating with a decisive influence on the leadership in the process of the Salvadorean people's social liberation, at other times it is identified with the Farabundo Martí FPL.

 What is the Popular Revolutionary Bloc?

Juan Chacón replied:

"The BPR is a revolutionary mass organization made up of popular organizations representing the various social sectors of the Salvadorean people in strategic unity revolving around the worker-peasant alliance, with proletarian hegemony....The BPR, founded on July 30, 1975, was the response to an urgent need posed as a logical consequence of deepening class struggle, the need for the people to have an organization that would battle resolutely in defense of their immediate and fundamental interests and for a democratic and revolutionary government. We could say that the BPR is the initial nucleus of the Mass Revolutionary Front.... Among its key principals are unity of action with other revolutionary and democratic forces in order to bring about the victory of popular revolution and advance

157

toward a just society with independence and freedom....The BPR also feels that all forms of struggle -
legal and illegal, peaceful and violent - are important
and necessary, but the important one, the focus of
attention, is the organized, combative struggle....This
fundamental form of mass struggle is part of our
strategy of prolonged popular war outlined in 1970 by
the Farabundo Martí Popular Liberation Forces."

▌2▐ What organizations make up the BPR?

General Secretary Chacón replied:
"The José Guillermo Rivas Trade Union Coordinating Committee and the Revolutionary Trade Union
Federation, which represent 60 unions; the Farm Workers Federation which is made up of the Christian
Federation of Salvadorean Peasants and Farm Workers
Union; the 21st of June National Association of Salvadorean Educators; the Revolutionary Secondary Students Movement; the 19th of July Revolutionary University Students; the 30th of July Revolutionary University Forces; the Slum Dwellers Union; the Neigh-
borhood and District Popular Committees; and the
Popular Culture Movement. A total of 100,000 Salvadoreans belong to these organizations and in the struggle for each of their sector's demands and in their
solidarity with other sectors struggle to achieve better
working conditions and further their awareness, organization and dedication to the cause of social revolution."

▌3▐ What are the objectives of the BPR?

"The first and most important objective is the
conquest of power and the implementation of a democratic and revolutionary government. Everything else
must be seen as a function of this, including among
other things: incorporating into the revolutionary struggle, in a mass, organized, combative manner, the different sectors of the population, as part of the strategy
of prolonged people's war; building up the Mass Revolutionary Front as the organizational and political
means for incorporating the broad masses into the
revolutionary struggle; creating the necessary organi-

zational tools - associations, unions, people's solidarity committees, revolutionary mass organizations, etc. - among different sectors of the people to promote the struggle for economic, political and social demands and for the prime goal, that is, uniting the peoples' struggle on a Central American level for revolution and the construction of a just society, coordinating this on a Latin American and world level; strengthening ties of friendship, solidarity and mutual aid with the revolutionary and democratic camp....Of course, all this stems from the worker-peasant alliance, with proletarian hegemony as the nucleus and basis for revolutionary unity among the various sectors and popular movements.

POLICY OF EXTERMINATION

During a meeting with the U.S. Chamber of Commerce in El Salvador, Ambassador Robert White said the objectives of U.S. policy in El Salvador consist in avoiding "at all costs" the victory of the Salvadorean people. This involves the elimination of the people's leaders, and Juan Chacón is one.

In the countryside the army and other repressive forces are undertaking joint operations and a large-scale offensive against towns which have become highly politicized.

The program drawn up by the CIA and the oligarchy "to restore social peace to El Salvador," which is being implemented by Colonels José Guillermo García, Nicolás Carranza, Eugenio Vides Casanova and - in spite of his apparent doubts - by Adolfo Arnoldo Majano, involves the murder of 250,000 to 300,000 Salvadoreans.

However, the program faces one insurmountable barrier: the organization and fighting spirit of a people determined to gain their future.